Once
A
Grenadier
Always
A
Grenadier

The Memoirs of Norman Wood

© Norman Wood 1997

ISBN 1 900880 10 5

Published by

OLD MILL BOOKS

DESIGN · PRINT · PUBLISH

3A Old Hall Mill Business Park, Alfreton Road, Little Eaton, Derbyshire DE21 5DL
Tel: 01332 835445 Fax: 01332 835443

Acknowledgments

To

Eric Edwards
Branch Secretary, Derby Branch
Grenadier Guards Association
for his invaluable help in preparing my memoirs

Lt Col P.H.M. Squires
R.C.M.P

Major P. Lewis
Grenadier Guards Regimental Archivist
for help given

Dedicated to my Wife Georgina
for her help and encouragement

Chapters

My Early Life

Return to Civvy Street

Return to The Colours

D-Day Return to France

Civvy Street

ABBREVIATIONS

NAVY

S.N.O.L.	Senior Naval Officer Landing
P.B.Mr.	Principal Beach Master
B.Mr.	Beach Master
A.B.M.	Assistant Beach Master

ARMY

U.L.O	Unit Landing Officer
M.L.O.	Military Landing Officer
A.M.L.O.	Assistant Military Landing Officer
F.O.O.	Forward Observation Officer (ARTY)

CRAFT

L.C.S	Landing Craft Support
L.S.T.	Landing Ship Tank
L.S.P.	Landing Ship Personnel
L.C.T	Landing Craft Tank
L.C.M.	Landing Craft Mechanised
L.C.P.	Landing Craft Personnel
L.C.A.	Landing Craft Assault L.C.V Landing Craft Vehicle

OTHERS

M.B.S.S	Main Beach Signal Station
P.T.A.	Personnel Transit Area
B.D.S.	Beach Dressing Station
T.V.T.A.	Tracked Vehicle Transit Area
W.V.T.A.	Wheeled Vehicle Transit Area
D.I.D.	Detail Issue Depot
O.B.D.	Ordnance Beach Detachment
P.O.W.	Prisoner of War
T.P.	Traffic Post
S.P.	Stragglers Post
P.O.L.	Petrol Oil and Lubricants
SUPS	Supplies
AMN	Ammunition
ORD.	Ordinance
A.D.S.	Advance Dressing Station
C.C.S.	Casualty Clearing Station
D4) D7)	Mark of Bulldozers
F.B.E	Folding Boat Equipment
D.V.P.	Drowned Vehicle Park
W.P.	WaterPoint
A.S.C	Advanced Surgical Complex

Chapter 1

My Early Life

I was born in Madeley Street, Derby on the 2nd of April 1910. My Father was employed by the old Midland Railway at Derby Station as a Controller. He lived his early years in Birmingham, where his mother had a small dressmaking business in the Small Heath area of the city. My mother Ethel Wood was born in Melton Mowbray, and married my father in 1908, she was one of five children born to Thomas Thorn a Colour Sergeant in the Grenadier Guards.

My uncle Arthur (Dad's brother) was one of the first members of The Royal Flying Corps. He was a pilot, and during the war rose to the rank of Captain. After the war he returned home to Halesowen, where he became an executive with The Dunlop Rubber Company.

My father was promoted to assistant Station Master at Ashby De La Zouch in 1912, and after 4 years, we moved to Measham were my father was again assistant Station Master. During this period the family lived in one of five railway cottages between Measham and Oakthorpe, the cottages were the only buildings between the two villages the nearest school was one and a half miles away, and in a time when the only way to get to school was to walk come rain or shine, and that at six years of age.

I remember my father trying to enlist in the Army in 1914 at the start of World War One, but was turned down, due to the fact that he was in a reserved occupation. At that time the railway was the fastest means of transporting troops and equipment around.

Life in the country did not appear to effect inhabitants of the villages as there was little news available, except through newspapers, and local gossip. The facts were brought home one day when the large house standing on crossroads south of the railway station was occupied by German prisoners of war. Each morning they were marched passed the front of the five cottages on there way to work on the local farms.

My family moved back to No 5 Alexandria Street, Derby in 1922 where my father transferred to the Fast Freight section as a Goods Guard based at Chaddesden sidings until his retirement in 1953.

I went to school at St. James Church, Dairyhouse Road, Normanton, Derby. The headmaster Mr. Sephton was a strict disciplinarian he encouraged sport and athletics. I played football for the school as a centre half until at the age of fourteen when I left and started work as a junior dispatch clerk in the night office on No1 platform at Derby Station. I later played football for LMS team in the old Wednesday League as centre half at the age of 15. I remember playing against Derby Butchers, Derby Co-op and Derby Tramways. In 1930, during the recession, I lost my job and joined the 3 million other people out of work, and at that time a means test was operative which meant that if either of my parents worked, I would not be able to claim any kind of help.

My grandfather who in the 1860's had been a Colour Sergeant with the Grenadier Guards advised me to join the regiment, he had served with the 1st Battalion during the South African and Egyptian campaigns. I joined the regiment on the 14th of March 1930. On my journey from London to Caterham I met up with two other recruits on their way to the depot, one was joining the Coldstream Guards and the other was for the Irish Guards. As we approached the guardroom at the depot I started getting butterflies in my stomach, I asked the sergeant if he could direct us to where we were supposed to go, he sent us to an assembly point near to the NAAFI. We were given a meal of rissoles which looked horrible and I refused them. The Sergeant Cook told me that if I was going to refuse these, then I should see what is to come, this food was a luxury compared to some of the food that we dish up here. I had saved some of the sandwiches that my mother had made for me on the journey and ate those instead of the rissoles. Afterwards we went go to our respective regiments.

We were then shown into a barrack room and assigned a bed by our trained soldier, (our squad instructor) he was Colour Sergeant Payne. During the next few days everything was done in double quick time; Reveille was at 06.00hrs and by 06.30hrs you had washed, shaved and been inspected ready for breakfast parade. At 0900 hrs. we were marched to the kit stores where we were issued with our uniforms of a canvas jacket and trousers with a stocking cap, this was the kit issued to recruits during training parades. We had been issued with our Karki uniforms but were not allowed to wear them until we had passed our basic marching parade tests. After we had put on our canvas jackets and trousers we had to fall in on the road outside the barrack block for inspection by our squad officer. He inspected our boots, uniform and general cleanliness. We then went on the parade ground and got our first of many lessons in marching. After the last parade of the day we were marched back to the barrack room and given the order to fall out, we were then told to get our knifes, forks, spoons and mugs and fall back in for tea parade. After tea we made our way back to the barrack room in double time and then we had to start cleaning our kit ready for the following day, this went on until 2000 hrs, after that we had 2.00hrs until lights out for recreation.

A PTI Sgt. came to the barrack room and asked for names of those who wanted to take up either boxing or gymnastics, I put my name forward for boxing. My first session in the gym was one I will never forget. I had stated to the Sgt. that I was in a boxing club in Derby before joining the army, and I had some boxing experience, the Sgt. soon changed that statement by giving me a sharp lesson in boxing, I have never forgotten. He then paired us up for two minute sessions of sparing to see what we could do, I was paired up with a huge lad from the Irish Guards after a few seconds I finished up on the floor again wondering what had hit me, everyone laughed but for my opponent he put his hand out to help me up, his name was Jack Doyle. He left the Irish Guards soon after that, when some boxing promoter paid for his release, so that he could box professionally. He later became heavy weight champion of Britain & Europe. I continued boxing with some success.

Some weeks later we were allowed out of barracks which we enjoyed, but before you could leave the depot you had to be inspected at the guardroom by the Sgt. of the Guard. I had taken part in a boxing match and had

Passing out photograph before joining the first battalion Grenadier Guards, at Wellington Barracks, July 1930.
Back Row: Guardsman N. Wood (Writer), J. Noble, T/S R. Mead, Gdsm. A. Coe, F. Sharp, G. Goss. Middle Row: Guardsman. R. Still, W. Riley, H. Charters, T. Skene, J. Conroy, J. Harrison, w. Sullivan, A. Day, S. Townes, J. Collings.
Front Row: Guardsman F. Dawson, T. Young, C.S.M. Brand, Sgt. F. Payne (Squad Instructor), Sgt. T. F. Teece Supt., Sgt. L Bates, C. G. Roberts, W. Allen.

gained a pair of black eyes, the following night I reported to the Sgt. of the Guard for inspection prior to going into town. When he saw my black eyes and said that I could not go into town looking like that, so about turn and back to the barrack room until they have gone. So there was no nights out on the town for me for two weeks.

We passed out of Caterham in July 1930 and were ordered to report to the 1st Battalion who were stationed at Wellington Barracks. We took up public duties until October, when the Battalion moved to Warley Barracks, prior to departing for a two year tour in Egypt.

On 19th November, the Battalion embarked from Southampton for Egypt on the troopship Somerset. When crossing the Bay of Biscay in thick fog, a near disaster was averted between the Somerset and a mystery ship that had come out from Lisbon, Portugal, it passed across the stern of the our ship within 50 yards. Two days out of Southampton we arrived in Gibraltar, were after a short stay we sailed on to Malta. On arriving in Valletta harbour, we anchored close to the aircraft carrier HMS Eagle, which later in World War II was sunk by German Submarines. The people of Malta were very friendly, and when the Somerset had docked, some Maltese youths dived into the sea to recover coins that had been thrown into the water by some of the troops on deck. Shore leave was allowed, and after refuelling the ship sailed on to Egypt.

Arriving at Alexandria in 1930, prior to entraining for Cairo

On the ninth day out of England we disembarked in Alexandria. During the journey from Malta we changed from heavy Khaki uniforms into drill kit. The heat was terrific, and the journey from Alexandria to Cairo was torturous due to a very slow train, and the fact that none of us were accustomed to the climate. The Battalion eventually arrived at Kasr el Nil barracks, which are situated on the East bank of the Nile.

I started life in Cairo in No4 Company but due to my Height (6'2") I was reassigned to The King's Company. The first week in barracks, other than guard duties, was taken up with debugging our iron beds, and erecting mosquito nets. Fatigues became part of our daily lives, and we had to clean the barracks from top to bottom before each morning parade. It took sometime to become acclimatised to the heat and revert to normal daily duties, there were also a number of improvements within the barracks that made life easier, these consisted of a cinema, swimming pool and a sports ground with a gymnasium, this was adjacent to the parade ground.

Reveille was at 05.00 hrs, because all parades, fatigues and work other than guard duties had to be completed before 12.30 hrs due to the heat of the afternoons. We were allowed to leave the barracks after 17.30 hrs, In my off duty periods I usually visited Ezbekia Gardens (a place were Garrison troops could relax) in the centre of Cairo. Army regulations forbade soldiers off duty to leave barracks singly, so everyone walked around in pairs due to security. White belts were worn with sheaved trenching tool helves attached (this was a tool used for digging a fox hole during a battle). This rule was enforced due to several Welsh Guardsmen being injured in several incidents during their occupation of Kasr el Nil barracks before the Grenadier Guards took over. The Ezbekia Gardens had a restaurant, games room and tennis courts. Guardsmen were welcomed by Nicolas Nicolaeds the Greek manager of Groupies Restaurant. His daughter was educated in England and worked in the Cairo Museum. We had to return to barracks by 22.00 hrs.

Educational classes were compulsory and part of training. Voluntary education was available to guardsmen after passing their third and second class examinations. The classes for the first class certificate were taken in the evenings by a member of the Army Education Corps.

I spent most evenings in the gymnasium, training for the company boxing team, and hoping to be selected to box for the Battalion Team. I played football and cricket at both company and battalion level. The first football match was against an Egyptian team at Kasr el Nil and the battalion was defeated by a score line of 1-6. This was put down to not being fully acclimatised, this seemed to be borne out in a rematch some months later when the battalion won 2-1.

In 1931 the Battalion moved to Abbasia under canvas, we were very close to the Pyramids and Sphinx on the Egyptian and Libyan border, Abbasia camp was also home to two other regiments, the King's Regiment and the 2nd Battalion South Staffordshire Regiment. During our stay at Abbasia, tactical situations and manoeuvres were carried out in the full extreme heat of the day and in full F.S.M.O. (Full Service Marching Order). The early exercises were for short periods, after acclimatising to the heat and desert (about a week) night exercise and longer distances were undertaken using compass bearings only, these became routine, but they also became tougher and required all to be in the peak of fitness.

Before returning to barracks at Kasr el Nil the battalion went to polygon ranges close to Heliopolis Airport for the annual shoot on the 1000 yards range, the range covered the following distances 100 yards, 200 yards, 300 yards and 500 yards. The Lee Enfield MkIII Rifle was used along with the Lewis Machine Gun. I was fair with the rifle, but was quite good with the Lewis gun, and became part of the King's Company shooting team in competitions.

Part of my service with the battalion in Cairo was as a member of the Regimental Police. The section consisted of six guardsmen and a provost sergeant, we were responsible for manning the one main gate, all vehicles and pedestrians had to past through the checkpoint as the perimeter consisted of an eight foot high spiked railing fence. During one particular period the Regimental Police, were asked to help the local Police with the drug problems that seemed to be on the increase due to the drug Hashish being bought into the country illegally by camel train traders. We were to observe and detain offenders, who were then handed over to the local police for sentence in court. The Commissioner of Police (an Englishman named Baker Bey), invited members of the Regimental Police to visit the dope pens at Adbin Caracol (prison), where the victims of dope carriers were interned. The whole place stank with human odour and individuals who looked like wrinkled monkeys, some of them close to death.

Life in barracks was not devoid of incidents, and on occasions tension and boredom caused friction. Tempers flared and as a result fights took place particularly if there were no N.C.Os present. The usual result was that someone would finish up with the odd black eye, although minor incidents were overlooked by all, no one would allow any serious fights to take place and would step in to stop them.

On rare occasions some guardsmen found it hard to accept strict discipline and the demands of the regiment. We had one in our midst. During our stay in Cairo it started with a series of thefts from personnel boxes in

Regimental Police duties, first battalion, Grenadier Guards, at the entrance to Kasr el Nil
barracks, Cairo Eygpt, 1931.

our barrack room. We had our suspicions of the one violent character in our barrack room, but could not prove anything until I purchased a new tin of black polish and put it in my box. I later found that it was missing and asked this character if he had been in my box and taken my polish, he admitted to taking it and gave it back to me. He showed no indication of guilt and said the "when you lose some kit, you pinch what you haven't got from someone else to replace it". I told him that if he ever stole from anyone again I would report him. He did not learn from this experience and was found in possession of stolen items from the married quarters whilst on fatigues. He was arrested, and appeared in front of the CO, and was given 28 day detention. He later returned to duty and re-offended by breaking into the Cookhouse and stealing rations. He was caught by the Sgt. Cook and was marched to the Guardroom, where he was placed in close arrest and again marched into C.O.s orders; but this time he got an unspecified sentence and never returned to the King's Company.

Trooping of the Colour, at Kasr el Nil barracks on June the 3rd 1931, on the occasion of His Majesty King George the fifth's birthday. The background building is the Cairo Museum.

In May 1931 we started rehearsals for the Trooping of the Colour, the Troop took place at Kasr el Nil barracks, on the occasion of the birthday of His Majesty King George V. The inspection of the troop was conducted by General Sir Peter Strickland, Commanding Garrison Troops in Cairo. **The actual troop details are shown in the Programme illustrated opposite:**

CELEBRATION IN CAIRO

OF THE

BIRTHDAY OF HIS MAJESTY KING GEORGE V

TROOPING of the COLOUR

AT

KASR-EL-NIL BARRACKS

ON

WEDNESDAY, 3rd JUNE 1931

BY

CAIRO INFANTRY BRIGADE

••○○◉○•••

Inspecting Officer :—

GENERAL Sir E. PETER STRICKLAND,
K.C.B., K.B.E., C.M.G., D.S.O.

COMMANDING BRITISH TROOPS IN EGYPT

Printed by C.E. Albertiri - Cairo.

Commanding the Parade —	Lieut.-Colonel J.S. HUGHES, M.C.
	1st. Bn. Grenadier Guards.
Major —	Major G. DAWES, D.S.O., M.C.,
	2nd. Bn. The South Staffordshire Regt.
Adjutant —	Captain W.H. Goschen,
	1st Bn. Grenadier Guards.

Troops on Parade

		Offrs.	O. Ranks.
No. 1 Guard. (Escort for the Colour) —	King's Company, 1st. Bn. Grenadier Guards.	3	64
	Commander - Captain C. W. Browning.		
	Lieutenant - 2/Lt. A.C. Huntington.		
	2/Lieutenant. - 2/Lt. Hon. C.L. Hamilton Russell.		
No. 2 Guard. —	1st. Bn. Grenadier Guards. Commander - Captain G. A. I. Dury, M.C.	3	64
No. 3 Guard. —	1st. Bn. The King's Regt. Commander - Major R. G. Tudor, M.C.	3	64
No. 4 Guard. —	1st. Bn. The King's Regt. Commander - Captain T. E. Chad, M.C.	3	64
No. 5 Guard. —	2nd. Bn. The South Staffordshire Regt. Commander - Captain S. F. Dixon, M.C.	3	64
No. 6 Guard. —	2nd. Bn. The South Staffordshire Regt. Commander-Captain G.L. Still.	3	64
Drums of 1st. Bn. Grenadier Guards.			32
Band and Drums of 1st. Bn. The King's Regt.			70
Band and Drums of 2nd Bn. The South Staffordshire Regt.			70
Troops keeping the Ground — 1st Bn. Grenadier Guards.			150
TOTAL		18	706

The History of Trooping the Colour

Trooping the Colours centres round the Colours of a Regiment, which are two in number; one being The King's Colours, the Symbol of the Crown to which a soldier's loyalty is due; the other the Regimental Colour, representing the spirit and traditions of the Regiment.

There is little doubt that Trooping the Colours had its origin in guard mounting parades of the past, and that it dates from the early eighteenth century or possibly seventeenth century.

The first official record is found in an order of May, 1775, issued by the Duke of Cumberland, the Commander-in-Chief.

Today the Regimental Colour only is being trooped in honour of His Majesty's Birthday. The ceremony is best described in five stages.

I. Preparation of the Parade.

The Guards are marched on and formed up by the Adjutant. Guard Commanders are moved out in front. This may originally have been the idea of handing over the guards to the officers. Guard Commanders being marched out may be a survival of when they used to collect to draw lots for different guards.

II. The Troop.

The ceremony proper now begins, the Band and Drums troop across the parade ground in slow time, returning in quick time.

III. Taking Over the Colour.

This is the oldest and most interesting part of the ceremony, probably dating from mediæval times.

When the standard was the rallying point of the Army, it was entrusted to a specially selected officer with much display by the men-at-arms.

In the present ceremony, the right hand guard forms the escort to the Colour and moves out to the tune of British Grenadiers.

The right of the line has been the place of honour since early times, when men fought with shields. The right was the unguarded, and, therefore, the vulnerable side. The senior régiment has a right to this position in the British Army, and eventually the Grenadier Company of the Guards was normally placed there. For this reason the British Grenadiers march is played. On arrival in position in front of the Colour, the Colour is handed over to the Colour Officer by the Regimental Sergeant Major as the representative of the former men-at-arms.

The escort present arms, the Sergeants on the outer flanks turning outward, and bringing their rifles to the Port. The reason for this is that the Sergeants used to be armed with a Halberd, or short Pike, with a cutting blade, and the Port is the first movement in Pike Drill for coming down from the shoulder, for attack or defence.

The significance of the Present Arms in the Salute is literally offering the weapon to a friend or stranger in token of trust. Consequently, while the escort to the Colour is technically defenceless, the Sergeants are protecting them from attack.

IV. Trooping the Colour.

The escort with the Colour now moves down the ranks of the Guards in slow time, and the Guards Present Arms, paying this tribute as a token of loyalty to the King's person.

V. The March Past.

The escort, with the Colour in its keeping, resumes its original position.

The Guards are formed up in Column, and, before moving off to their duties, march past in slow and quick time, displaying to the onlookers the Symbol they hold in such high esteem.

Thus ends the ceremony, which is one of the most impressive in the Army, and still survives to uphold the traditions of the past.

Programme of Music
TO BE
PERFORMED

General Salute   " Cavalry Brigade "

INSPECTION OF THE LINE

Slow March   May Blossom

THE TROOP

Slow Troop	The Colours.
Quick Troop	The Contemptibles
Escort for the Colour	The British Grenadiers
Trooping the Colour	The Grenadiers March

THE MARCH PAST
(In slow Time)

1st. Bn. Grenadier Guards	The Duke of York
1st. Bn. the Kings Regt.	Mollendorf
2nd Bn. Staffordshire Regt.	The 80th.

(In quick time)

1st. Bn. Grenadier Guards.	The British Grenadiers
1st. Bn. the Kings Regt.	Heres to the maiden of bashful fifteen
2nd. Bn. Staffordshire Regt.	Come lasses and lads

Riots broke out in Palestine, and the Palestine Police Force could not control the situation and called for army support. A detachment from the Grenadier Guards was flown out by the Royal Air Force at Heliopolis. The incidence occurred between Jews and Arabs in Jerusalem at the wailing wall, but was soon brought under control, and the detachment returned to Cairo within a few days.

Royal Air Force troop carrier prior to the departure of Grenadier guards to Palestine. 30th July 1931

During the winter of 1931/32, a football match was arranged between Officers and other ranks, most of the latter being members of the battalion football team in the Cairo league. The result was never in doubt, but on the day it turned out to be a comedy farce. The Officers turned out in all types of kit. At half time the Officers were losing by 6 - 0. Their goal keeper never moved at even the simplest of shots at goal, and when Colonel Hughes playing at centre forward shouted, "Teddy you are there to stop them you know". Teddy dressed in a multicoloured shirt and wearing cricket pads & gloves, replied "what's the bloody net for"! I cannot remember what the final score was, but it was a great game.

At the end of 1931, a contingent of Guardsmen, NCO's and Officers arrived to replace those who had finished their tour of duty with the battalion and were to return home for demob.

17

I started to keep a diary in 1932, recording my life in the regiment, and what happened in the day-to-day affairs of the regiment. The first event was a route march to acclimatise the new arrivals from the U.K.

During my first year in Cairo particular emphasis was made to clean up the image of the Brigade of Guards with civilians, due to the conduct of other regiments that had been to Cairo before, as they had almost caused riots. Throughout the first year the conduct of the battalion had resulted in praise from the Cairo City Police and the High Commissioner. There were however some isolated incidents, due to the volatile nature of the city towards the army that demanded a lot of restraint on the part of the guardsmen. One such incident took place on the 16th January 1932, when three guardsmen were attacked by 16 Ghaffirs in the Pharssie-Bouton area of Cairo. Regimental Police, under Sgt. Cutts, were called out to quell the disturbance. Guardsmen Grimes and Frost sustained cuts and bruises, Frost lost his trenching tool helve during the incident.

On the 26th January 1932, the battalion left Kasr-el-Nil for Mena Camp, for desert exercises, this included the replacements from the U.K. who had not yet properly acclimatised themselves, and within a short period of time were enduring a strength sapping march on sand. One junior officer became distressed and handed over command to the Company Sergeant Major. He explained that he would return to camp on a set compass bearing, and the company marched on without him. On returning to camp at 1600 hrs. The officer had still not returned, and there was concern for his safety. At 1800 hrs. the young lieutenant arrived in camp on a donkey led by an Arab. The officer had his boots tied around his neck and was sucking an orange. He was seen arriving by the Adjutant, who made an unspecified remark to the young officer, who showed no sign of remorse. He spent the next few weeks inspecting breakfast parades as a punishment for his behaviour.

On the 3rd of February, the foundation stone was laid by King Fuad of Egypt, for the new Kasr-el-Nil bridge over the river Nile. Two life size gilt lions from the old bridge were restored to grace the entrance to the new bridge.

On Thursday the 3rd of March, Lieutenant Colonel The Viscount Gort, VC, CBE, DSO, MVO, MC. arrived at Kasr-el-Nil at 1715 hrs. in civilian clothes no doubt in connection with the proposed visit of ex-King Alfonso. On Saturday the 5th March, Ex-King Alfonso with His Excellency the High Commissioner; General Officer Commanding Cairo Garrison; Air Vice Marshal and Brigadier Robbie held a conference in the Officers mess, Viscount Gort presided at the meeting. Monday the 7th March 1932,

Ex-King Alfonso departing from the Officer's Mess Kasr el Nil barracks, 1932.
In attendance are Major Wiggins, Captain Goulburn, Colonel Hugh and Viscount Gort.

ex King Alfonso inspected the Battalion (and was photographed with the Kings Company) on parade at Kasr-el-Nil Barracks.

Saturday the 9th April 1932, Guardsman O'Neil received 14 days confined to barracks for lying about an Egyptian being knocked down whilst he was driving Captain Brownings car.

I was a member of the Guild of St George, and I attended meetings of the organisation, dealing with social activities. Major Magney, and Captain Ellison agreed on a suggestion for various trips to take place during our stay in Cairo. The trips would be organised at company level. Places to be visited and dates of travel would be arranged at future meetings. The first trip was by the Kings Company to Memphis on the 27th April and later to Saqqhra. During April, summer time routine was again introduced with reveille at 0500 hrs. so that parades would be completed before the heat of the day took effect.

The Trooping of the Colour for His Majesty King George V birthday was arranged to take place on the 3rd June at Gezira Club's ground on Gezira Island, with all units of the Cairo Garrison taking part. The Trooping of the Colour was by Kings Company, Grenadier Guards who provided the Escort, The battalion also provided No.2 Guard, with the Kings Own Royal Regiment Providing No's 3 and 4 Guard, and the 2nd Battalion South Staffordshire Regiment providing No's 5 and 6 Guards.

The music for the Troop was provided by the following:-

> 12th Royal Lancer (dismounted)
> 17th/21st Lancers (mounted)
> 14th/20th Hussars (dismounted)
> Drums of the 1st Battalion Grenadier Guards
> Drums of the first Battalion Kings Own Regiment
> Drums of the South Staffordshire Regiment

Troops keeping ground were from 1st Battalion Grenadier Guards. The Royal Air Force provided the fly pass, with 208 Squadron and No 45 Bomber Squadron. The estimated number of people attending was between 10,000 to 15,000. After the troop was over, I together with other members of the Kings Company went on two weeks leave to Sidi Gaber, on the outskirts of Alexandria. The holiday camp was under canvas, by the sea, and was in complete contrast to the sand of the desert. The days were spent swimming and visiting the Gloria Skating Rink in the evening.

Photograph of Kings company Lewis Gun Team, photograph taken at Polygon Camp, 1931

We returned to Kasr-el-Nil and reported for duty on the 18th of June. On the 31st July we again returned to polygon ranges for the annual live firing. My rifle marks improved from my 1931 score, and my Lewis Gun tally remained the same. I was again selected to shoot for the company in competitions with the small bore 22 rifle. On the 2nd September the Battalion shooting team entered the Command Competition at polygon ranges, and won the team event, I won an individual award in the automatic weapons series. On the 5th September I was leading on points in the second of three rounds when I was forced to retire with a broken right thumb. Guardsman Jackson of No 4 Company won the event.

On the 14th September I was on duty with the Regimental Police, when we received orders to go to Babel-el-Hadid were a private was being held for the murder of a sergeant from the 12th Lancers. The soldier was arrested and later handed over to the Military Police.

On the 25th of September, the South Staffordshire Regiment left Cairo enroute for Bangalore, India. They where replaced by the Royal Ulster Rifles, who arrived in Alexandria the same day. Brigadier Robbie inspected the Battalion, in readiness for the G.O.C inspection on the 22nd of October. After the G.O.Cs inspection he sent a message of congratulations to all on an excellent turn out and on the good conduct of the battalion during its tour of duty with the Cairo Garrison.

Kings Company, 1st Battalion Grenadier Guards, at the Barrage, 1932

On the 28th of October the battalion left Kasr-el-Nil barracks for Port Said and next day embarked on the troopship Nevasa to return the United Kingdom. The Sea was very rough until we docked in Malta on the 31st. The ship left Malta on the 1st November, again the weather was bad and the sea rough, many on board went down with sea sickness. The weather eased as we arrived at Gibraltar at 1100 hrs. on the 3rd November. After refuelling we left Gibraltar one of our number died, and off Cape Finesterre, the ships engine were stopped. The captain spoke on the tannoy and asked for a general assembly on deck for a burial at sea service. The ship then returned to its course and continued on to Southampton arriving in port on the 7th November. The Battalion returned to Warley Barracks, Brentwood, Essex in November 1933.

I finished my tour of duty with the colours and was discharged from the regular army and transferred to army reserve.

CHAPTER 2

Return to Civvy Street

I applied to join the Derbyshire County Constabulary and after a preliminary medical and educational examination I was finally granted recruit training as a police officer at Irongate, Derby. This was the training centre for police recruits from Derbyshire, Northamptonshire, Cambridge and the Isle of Eley. The initial police training was controlled by Superintendent Rogers, assisted by Inspector Hudson. The training was over three months, consisting of technical and physical ability of police officers in law & order situations with the general public. The syllabus included lectures on police activities, procedures in law, drill periods, ju jitsu, and in the later stages of training mock courtroom exercises, where evidence of incidents was heard and points awarded for proficiency. Swimming lessons were taken and certificates in life saving had to be obtained before passing out examinations. My assessment both educationally and physically was approved by the Chief Constable and I was transferred to the Buxton Division as a police constable.

During my probationary period, I was accompanied on the beat by a sergeant, or senior police officer, and was involved in incidents of a domestic nature. One incident occurred during night duty, when three unoccupied dwellings were broken into on the Macclesfield Road. I had checked these houses out earlier between 11.00 pm and 1.00 am, and found no problems. I was ordered to attend the investigation during the morning by a detective constable and found out from the neighbours that the break-ins had occurred at about 3.00 am that morning. The method of entry was through the three larder windows, they were about 9" by 12" in size, far to small for a grown man, and it was believed that a child had been pushed through to open the doors. Some months later a gang of three men and a woman were arrested in Blackpool, they asked for the three offences at Buxton to be taken into consideration. Later it was discovered that the woman was small and very slender and she had been passed through the larder windows.

I was on point duty at the junction of Terrace Road and Spring Gardens, when a Rolls Royce car stopped outside a shop in Spring Gardens, the driver got out, and went into a shop leaving the car some three feet away from the pavement causing a huge build up of traffic. I left my post on point duty, and went to the shop, as I entered the shop, I saw that the driver was making a purchase. I approached him and informed him that he would have to return to his car and move it has it was causing an obstruction. He became very angry and shouted " I will move it when I'm ready, and don't be so bloody impertinent". I again warned him that if he didn't move his car immediately, I would report him. His reply was, "I know you superior and will report you". He left the shop, and drove off. About half an hour later the shift inspector relieved me from point duty and told me to report to the superintendent at the police station. I reported to the charge office sergeant, who said that the superintendent was engaged with the man who from his description was the owner of the Rolls Royce. I heard his voice shouting some indistinguishable words at the superintendent and he then left the office slamming the door behind him. The station sergeant announced my presence and I was marched in. The superintendent (Martin Else) spoke with a broad Derbyshire accent said " I have had a complaint about thee lad, I have heard what he had to say, now I want your side of the story". I repeated the circumstances and waited for some admonishment, but I was rather taken back when he said, "all reet lad get back on your beat".

Some months later during the winter months, I was passing the local cinema, when I saw the same Rolls Royce, parked without lights. I asked the attendant in the foyer, who stated that he knew the owner of the car, and that the vehicle had been parked outside the cinema for some time. I approached the man who was accompanied by his wife as he left the cinema, and drew his attention to the fact that he had no obligatory lights at the front or rear of his car. I informed him that he would be reported for the offences, and asked for his driving licence and insurance documents, to which his reply was, "you will have to come to my house if you want to see them". I informed him that it was not my duty to chase around after him and issued him with an HORT 1, and told him he must produce his documents within the period demanded by law, he stated that he would produce his documents at Buxton police station. He was later summons to appear at Buxton Court, where he should have been chairman of the bench on the date of the hearing. He was found 'guilty' on all charges; for no lights, not producing his driving licence and certificate of insurance within the allotted time. He was severely rebuked by the stand-in chairman, he was fined £5.00 on each of the four charges.

In certain circumstances it can be very embarrassing for police officers, this happened to me one night. I was out on patrol at around 2.00 am in the morning, I was checking shops and other business premises in Spring Gardens, Buxton, when a man informed me that there was a drunken naked woman lying in the grassed area near the Crescent. I asked him to accompany me to the Crescent, on arrival I saw the woman lying on her side. She had been drinking what smelt like methylated spirits. I looked around for her clothes without success, so together with the man who first reported the incident we managed to get her to the police station. Her clothes were later found near the pavilion garden entrance. She was charged with being drunk and incapable, and was fined. Records revealed that she had on several occasions been convicted for similar offences.

At that time Buxton Division provided holiday relief for the police officer at Dove Holes. I was detailed for this duty, and on one particular night duty I stood on the railway bridge close to the railway station when I saw a man break into the gangers hut. I slid down the bank close to the bridge and heard noises coming from the hut, and a few minutes later a man emerged from the interior carrying an overcoat, and a railway lamp. I informed him that I had seen him breaking into the hut and that he was under arrest, he said that he was only trying to make a few bob. He gave his name as Albert Walters of no fixed abode. He was later conveyed to Buxton Police Station and charged with the offences. He had an history of burglary and other none violent offences. He later appeared in court and was sentenced to six months imprisonment. After sentence I escorted him to Strangeways prison Manchester. He was quite a character and he told me that although he was only 42 he had spent 18 years in various prisons around the country and had several aliases. On arrival at Strangeways, he was recognised by the head warder who said "what name is it this time?" Walter was quite a likeable rogue.

Some months later I was transferred to Whitwell, a mining village in Eckington Division. The outgoing constable, was transferring to Buxton. He told me that he had applied for transfer, due to difficulties that had arisen between him and the mining community. He had a university education and found that his life had been handicapped by his failure to come to terms with what he described as the class of people in the village, who he thought were out to get him.

I found lodgings with Mr. and Mrs. Slaney, who agreed that I could use my room for the writing of police reports and any other police business, other than holding prisoners, and have the customary sign as a police house above the entrance. I found duties in a village far different from Buxton. The hours worked on the beat were irregular and domestic issues were common. I had to visit farms in the area and make reports on the movements of all farm animals to and from markets, these had to be completed and passed onto headquarters under the Ministry of Agriculture & Fisheries Act.

A few weeks after my arrival, and during a carol service in the village square, I was called out to an incident where two drunken men had assaulted some of the carol singers. It was during the early evening, and found two men, one of whom I recognised as a local miner, stumbling about amongst a crowd of locals. I got hold of the coat collars of both men and struggled towards the home of the man who I recognised. I had gone about one hundred yards when the stranger slipped out of my grasp and fell against a wall. He lay stretched out when I received assistance from a member of the carol singing team who had followed me. He held the local drunk, whilst I picked the man up of the pavement. I eventually arrived at the home of the local drunk, his wife took both of them into the house. The man who had fallen against the wall had got a large bruise on the left cheek near his eye but otherwise he was unhurt. The wife of the miner was concerned about my reporting the incident, but as I had no complaints or report of injuries I said that no further action would be taken. Mr. Slaney informed me after a visit to the local miner's welfare club the following dinner time, he had met Sunny Lee who was a professional boxer from Leeds. He was supporting a black eye and swollen face. He stated that the local copper had knocked him out the night before during a drunken fight in the street, while he and his miner friend had been jeering at the local carol singers. From that day on I never had any trouble with the local mining community and when I met any miner in the street they gave me a wide berth or talked about the time I knocked out Sunny Lee.

As a Police Constable stationed at Whitwell, in 1935. The photograph was taken at the commemoration of the 1st World War in November of that year.

The background shows the flag of the British Legion's local branch en route to church on the 15th anniversary since the formation of the British Legion

One further incident took place at Whitwell during the annual visit of a fair. I was due on patrol between 9.00 pm and 1.00 am, when my section sergeant visited me at about 7.00 pm and requested that I accompany him to what he described as an incident at the fairground. He went on to say that two men who he had recently reported for theft of timber had been following him around the fairground with intent to intimidate him. On arrival at the fairground the sergeant pointed out the two men, I recognised them as being two mining brothers from Whitwell, and they continued following us around. I told the sergeant that I would go and talk to them about their conduct, as I had known the Brown brothers for sometime, and felt that their actions were totally out of character. I approached them and asked for an explanation and was told that one night they had been leaving the pit and noticed a length of timber in the roadside close to a building site and had picked it up, as they did so the sergeant had popped out of the bushes and reported them with theft. I told them that by harassing the sergeant they were doing themselves no good at all. I advised them to go home and think about how to clear their names. I then left for my lodgings. At 11.00 pm the same evening I was met by the sergeant who asked me to accompany him part way to his section headquarters at Cresswell, we passed the cottage where the two brothers lived. He bid me good night just beyond the cottages and I continued with my patrol.

I served almost two years at Whitwell, and played cricket for the local village team, that included Tom Mitchell and Douglas Hounsfield who later played for Derbyshire and Nottinghamshire respectively.

In 1936 I was transferred to Clowne, also part of the Eckington Division. My first assignment came whilst on night duty when I was called to the scene of an accident between a cyclist, and a newspaper delivery van. The cyclist, on his way to Oxcorft colliery, was lying in the road in a prone position surrounded by other miners who were also on their way to the same colliery. I checked the body for a pulse and found none. The van was on the correct side of the road, and the statements taken made it apparent that the cyclist had lost control of his machine. His head had been in contact with the driving mirror of the van causing instant death to the cyclist. I later had to visit his home, and inform his parents of his death. This I know was one of the worst things which I, or for that matter, any police officer, has to do in his career.

Domestic problems in a mining district occupies a considerable amount of police time. I was returning to my lodgings at midnight, after being signed off by the station sergeant, I was walking down the high street, in appalling weather, when I passed a shop doorway and found two women hiding there in a distraught state. I spoke to the two women and noticed that the older woman had blood coming from her nose. I enquired as to why they were in the doorway, and who had caused the nose bleed and bruising. The younger woman, I found was in fact the daughter of the injured woman. I again asked what had happened, and the elder woman stated that her husband had attacked her and thrown her and her daughter out of the house. I accompanied both women back to their house in the West Lea area, which I later learned was notorious for violence. On reaching the house, I found that the front and back doors were locked and bolted and all the windows had been fastened down. I could not leave these two women out of their house in this weather, so with the mothers permission, I slid back the catch on the kitchen window and climbed through, I opened the back door for the women. There was no sign of the woman's husband down stairs. Both women were still in fear of further violence from the husband and father if he were still in the house. I was asked to look around the house just to make sure he had gone. I went up stairs into the back bedroom and received a violent blow in the lower part of my back, which sent me staggering forward, I regained my balance, and saw a man who from the description given by the wife was the husband. He came at me again but this time I was ready for him and defended myself. I then went at my attacker and got an arm lock on him, I forced him down stairs and warned him against further aggression and released him. He immediately picked up a brass fender from the fireplace, lifted it above his head and swung it at me. I raised my arm but could not prevent him hitting me with the fender and as he did so the end broke off. He dropped the fender and tried to punch me in and around the face. At this point I though I must stop this man before any more harm should come to me or the two women. I struck the man who fell to the floor pulling the table cloth off the table and all the contents from the table as well which included his half eaten meal. He struggled to his feet and threw a flat iron at me which missed me and wiped out all the ornaments on the sideboard. I managed to overcome him and asked for an explanation of his behaviour, his reply was "The old cow asked for it".

I then informed him that the injuries his wife and daughter had received were bodily harm and he was being arrested for assaulting a police officer in the course of his duty. I took him to the police station, where he was officially charged, he was locked up for the night and would appear before a special court the following day. He was found guilty, and before sentence, his previous 33 convictions where taken into account, mainly of violence, three of which were for attacks on police officers, and one of three years for incest. He was sentenced to 6 months imprisonment. On his release I was told that he was likely to seek vengeance on the person who had sent him down. I was on patrol in a remote part of town when I saw him leave the recreation ground and come towards me. There was no one about, as I approached him, I thought if he lives up to his reputation, this would make an ideal opportunity for him to seek revenge. I walked closer but as the gap closed he dropped his eyes to the ground and scuttled passed me without any problem, I never had any further trouble from him.

To finish this story, I was approached by a young man, some months later. He told me he was the son of the man I had put into prison. He said that he was a professional footballer and played for West Bromwich Albion. He offered his thanks to me for dealing with the circumstances, which resulted in his father being imprisoned. He told me that his mother and sister had been subjected to his fathers brutality for many years, but now his father seems to have settled down to home life.

CHAPTER 3

Return to The Colours

In 1939, at the outbreak of World War II. I was called up to service with my old Battalion in the Grenadier Guards, first for training at Wellington barracks and Pirbright, before further training on tracked vehicles with the mortar platoon of Kings company at Yeovil. At the end of September 1939, we sailed from Southampton on the troop ship St. Helier landing at Cherbourg, France. Spending the night bivouacked on the railway station. On the last day of September we marched (full pack order) 22 Kilometres, eventually arriving at Lille and billeted near the Belgium border. The Battalion did exercises and battle practice near Metz, and eventually between the Maginot Line, where German troops recce patrols were often seen which was near the Siegfied Line. The Battalion remained in static positions doing revetting and trench digging in snow and icy conditions.

Photograph taken January, 1940 at Lille, France, after return from manoeuvres north of Metz with Kings Company, 1st Battalion Grenadier Guards.

In March 1940, I was with two other Grenadiers who had been regular policemen in civvy street and were ordered to report to BEF Headquarters for special duties to Lord Gort, who was the Army Commander of the British Expeditionary Force at Arras. Lord Gort was an ex-Grenadier and had requested that three grenadiers with police experience be sent to act as his personnel bodyguards, so I and the two other guardsmen were then transferred to the Corps of Military Police for this specific purpose.

On the 10th of May 1940, the Germans attacked through Sedan in the French Sector, and through Rotterdam in Holland. BEF Headquarters moved into Belgium and were attacked on numerous occasions by Junker 87 and 88 fighter bombers. At Popering, Hazebrook and Ypres, Dornier bombers raised buildings to the ground making roads almost impassable, the progress of military personnel was hampered by columns of refugees. On one occasion German fighters attacked a HQ group of vehicles moving through northern France with my unit of military police. At the time we were halted by refugees occupying the whole of the road, and in consequence all military units were ordered to take cover in ditches on either side of the road, I went to ground in the ditch together with a number of refugees. The raid was over within a few minutes it was then I found an elderly man lying in the ditch a few yards from were I stood. He made no response telling him the raid was over, so I checked his pulse and found that he was dead. His identity card revealed that he was from Breda in Holland so to prevent valuables including Dutch Guilders from being stolen I took particulars from his identity card, which I left on the body and handed the property to a captain at BEF Headquarters.

On the 28th of May, Headquarters moved from Wahagnes in Northern France to La Panne on the Belgium border, being attacked on several occasions by German aircraft. I remained with Headquarters BEF until the 30th of May, when I was told that I would be part of a section from Headquarters that would form a rear guard operation, and later that day received orders to proceed to Dunkirk to assist in the orderly evacuation of troops from the beaches. On arrival in Dunkirk it was like a living hell. Every building appeared to be on fire, a pall of black smoke blowing like fog across the beaches. Although air raids became more frequent, there appeared to be no panic amongst troops waiting to be taken off, (probably due to the fact that most of the men were too tired to care). During the morning of the 30th the West Mole was untenable due to direct hits from German aircraft, but destroyers, together with all types of small vessels continued to use the East Mole to take both French and British troops. Queues were formed so that small craft were able to load a safe number for the trip to England, the whole exercise was frequently jeopardised by incessant air raids and shelling. By noon on the 31st of May the whole beach area was littered with debris from ships that had been sunk, wounded men both French and British who we sought to get of the beach first when transport ships and boats became available. Exhausted troops, constantly harried by German aircraft, and on arrival on the beach, gained confidence by the sight of Red Caps directing divisional soldiers to arriving ships and other craft taking them to possible safety, away from the carnage ashore.

At least 5 men and several members of the military police were killed or wounded by shelling or bombs in the latter days of the evacuation. On my section of beach, the majority of troops were waiting their turn in silence, even the wounded attended by RAMC personnel were given a degree of priority. In these circumstances it was essential that control and calm must be exercised to effect the evacuation of as many troops as possible. To prevent panic, the attitude of the Military Police achieved a high peak of service and self sacrifice.

My last duties at Dunkirk during the mornings of the 1st and 2nd of June, involved checking the dunes of the East beach for soldiers who were either asleep or unwilling to get to safety, and to get them to a part of the beach where they could embark as the boats came to their rescue. I eventually received orders to go to the East Mole where together with a group of French soldiers embarked on a British destroyer for England.

I was granted leave some three weeks after my return to England and on arriving home I found that my wife had received notification that I had been reported missing at Dunkirk. I learned that my brother Ron, who I had last seen in France, serving with the Royal Engineers had been evacuated through La Panne, and was on his way to an undisclosed destination. My youngest brother Keith who at the age of 17 had volunteered for service with the Royal Navy. During the latter stages of the war in Europe, I learned that Ron had served in Burma, and Keith had been on the aircraft carrier Indefatigable on convoy duties to Mumansk and Arc Angel in Russia, and after had been on the same aircraft carrier with Admiral Nimitz's task force against the Japanese at Okinawa in the Pacific.

After a leave at home, I joined a Military police unit on the outskirts of Southampton where the area was under constant attacks from bombers, causing extensive damage to property and loss of life. On one occasion, I was off duty and went to the cinema in East Gate, during the film sirens went and before the cinema could be evacuated the whole of the back of the building caved in. My colleagues from the Military police unit, and myself, assisted civil police in extricating injured civilians and some service personnel from the rubble. Outside the cinema the fire brigade were tackling many fires from burning buildings.

In January 1941, my wife gave birth to our son, and I was granted leave. Snow was falling in Derby when I arrived home, she was staying at my parents home, but appeared to be very depressed. On the following day, she told me that she would like to visit our home at Buxton Road, which had remained unoccupied since the outbreak of war. I had promised my parents to shift snow from paths round their house, whilst my wife was away, so as she seemed in a good frame of mind, she left my parents home early so as to return some time before lunch. She had not returned for lunch, so later during the afternoon I went to Buxton Road. Entering the dining room I found my wife lying on the carpet. She had a small Biretta pistol in her right hand and then I noticed a small pool of blood which stained the carpet. I checked the pulse and found that she was dead. I called the police. They took statements which I acknowledged the weapon was a souvenir brought back from Dunkirk. At the inquest, the coroner returned a verdict of death by suicide, whilst she was suffering from acute post natal depression.

After the funeral my parents agreed to look after my son and I returned to my unit. For some weeks afterwards I felt the loss of my wife was seriously effecting my position as a senior NCO of the company. My RSM and company commander were very understanding and supportive. They suggested that a transfer to another company may prove to beneficial, so I was eventually transferred to Mytchett camp for training recruits. I spent a few weeks at Mytchett camp Aldershot, but later joined Southern command headquarters where General Montgomery was in charge of 1st Corps. The 1st Corps Headquarters which were near to Salisbury, and my section was responsible for vehicle movements in and out of headquarters, and checking of passes and permits.

On one occasion one of my corporals reported that he had stopped General Montgomery's car as it entered headquarters and the General was in the car. He asked the General to produce his Identity Card, which was produced and inspected. I remonstrated with the corporal, and about 6.00 pm I was called to headquarters, and was informed of the incident. The staff captain referred to the fact that the General had been stopped and asked to produce his identity card (A.F. 2606), and to my surprise was requested to compliment the corporal, as the driver of the car had entered headquarters with the Generals flag furled, denoting that he was not in the car, whereas the flag should have been unfurled showing that he was in his car. I do not know whether it was a test of security, or whether the driver had forgotten to unfurl the flag, but two days later a commendation appeared in Part 2 orders, on the instruction of the General.

The headquarters of the British Expeditionary force at La Petite Place, Arras, 1939.

Photograph taken during manoeuvres near the Maginot Line, France, with Kings Company
1st Battalion Grenadier Guards, January, 1940.

Dunkirk after the evacuation of troops from the beaches. Photograph taken at the end of June, 1940.

This photograph taken after the evacuation of allied troops from the beach at Dunkirk, shows the vehicles assembled to form a bridge at high water, enabling troops to escape to waiting ships. The East mole having been destroyed by bombs from Junkers 87 & 88 Dive Bombers.

Place Jean Bart - Buildings demolished after raids by Junkers 87 & 88, during the evacuation from Dunkirk.

Dunkirk, abandoned wrecks of ships after the evacuation of troops, June, 1944.

During the period at Corp Headquarters, General Montgomery had Headquarters staff doing a seven mile cross country run, staff running on Wednesday being excused on Thursday and vice versa. The General ran both days. One incident of Monty's attitude was demonstrated as a disciplinarian when a roll call on the Wednesday run revealed the absence of an officer who was missing parade. The officer concerned turned out on Thursday in gym kit prepared to run, and was asked to explain his absence on the previous day, for which he had no answer. Monty held up the parade and ordered the officer to change into duty uniform, complete with Sam Brown equipment, the run taking place with the officer running with Montgomery and the Brigadier running behind. It was a hot day and the officer concerned was a pitiable sight on his return from the run. The General neither smoked or drank alcohol and was a keen disciplinarian. He appeared to direct his attention for perfection of his officers and ranks, expecting and getting effective response from all units. As a senior NCO I sat in on many conferences when the General officiated. The conferences were always directed by a no smoking rule, for anyone who did smoke did so outside the conference building, five minutes before meetings took place.

During July 1941, I trained several squads at Aldershot under extreme pressure, and then applied for a transfer to an operational unit which was approved. About a month later, I received orders to transfer to a holding unit at Edinburgh Castle, where I found that the RSM was WO1 Ward (an Ex Coldstream Guards NCO). During the waiting period before transfer to operational duties, I supervised the military police patrols on Princess Street, from the Haymarket to Leith Walk and the Docks Area.

The RSM & myself eventually received orders to proceed to Rothes, near Elgin, to reorganise a Military police unit of the 52nd (mountain) Division. The unit had been declared inefficient and negligent. In order to allow the RSM an interval to complete his commitments at Edinburgh I proceeded him by a few days, to the unit which was The Divisional Provost Company. The unit was housed in a large country house, and I was appalled at the state of the unhygienic situation that I found. The majority of the men were unshaven, the smell was that of a pigsty and no badges of rank were to be seen. I asked where the Warrant Officer in charge of the unit was and a scruffy individual was indicated playing cards with three others. The soldier stated that he was CSM Bradshaw, so I referred to the fact that he wore no uniform to indicate rank, and that he was involved in a game of cards with money, was contrary to good order & military discipline (as required by Kings regulations), I also drew his attention to the state of the sleeping arrangements of the men, as there were no beds in the habitat. Palliasses were strewn haphazard in several rooms of the building. They were in a filthy condition many required repair. I advised CSM

Bradshaw to get the place tidied up before RSM Ward arrived, and warned that severe disciplinary action would result, if matters did not improve.

RSM Ward arrived a few days later, and placed all NCO's above that of Lance Corporal under arrest, until replacements for their respective ranks were transferred from the holding unit. The RSM had everyone in the unit cleaning the house, each room being hosed with disinfectant water, and the palliasses removed from the building and burned. All uniforms were taken outside into the yard and sprinkled with DTT to kill any infestation.

The RSM and myself obtained civilian billets with a Mrs. Robertson in the High Street, Rothes, and during the following week Sgt. McNab, (ex Scots Guards), Sgt. Fraser and Sgt. Harris both ex Grenadier Guards reported for duty as replacements for the WO2 and Sgts previously under arrest. Investigation on how the unit failed to fulfil the standards required by the Corps of Military Police revealed that the unit was formed in 1940 from the Territorial Army and most of the men had very little training. One of the soldiers told me that he and the other soldiers of the company were from the Corbals slum district of Glasgow and were unused to the strict discipline of Military police. For three months senior NCO's and the RSM worked 14 hours a day in order to bring the company up to Military Police standards. Reveille was at 06.00 hrs concluding at 08.00 hrs. The orderly Sergeant was responsible for the soldiers roll call at breakfast parade (06.30 hrs with everyone washed and shaved). Breakfast at 07.00 to 08.00 hrs preparation for drill parade at 09.00 hrs until 10.00 hrs (this was in full pack order for the first 4 weeks).

Current affair lectures, Physical Training, and other parades as detailed in Part 1 orders until after the tea interval 16.30 to 17.30 hrs, 18.00 to 20.00 hrs detailed equipment cleaning; 20.00 till 22.00 hrs leisure period within the boundaries of the billets area. No passes were permitted throughout the period in which strict discipline was enforced. Anyone trained at the Guards Depot as a recruit, will understand the rigours entailed in order for a soldier to be faultless in behaviour and turn out, before allowing the general public to see them. After three months and many hours of what the army term jankers the response was very satisfactory.

The 52nd Division were joined by a Norwegian Brigade and the whole division went on full mountain exercises and manoeuvres including mountain climbing and ski training. The Norwegians were experts. The exercises took place in the Caingorms from October 1942 till March 1943 in the Aviemore area. The first ski slopes were designed by the Norwegians who were skiing on heather before the snow came. The training was intense and contained extreme fitness similar to arctic training. There were numerous casualties as a result, but the worst feature of such training was the food, which consisted of packs of Pemican, this was part of the rigid survival conditions expected of every man in the division. The division, we later learned were being trained for operational duties in Norway, which were later abandoned.

I remained with the division until the spring of 1943 and felt that I would best serve my country by transferring to an active operational unit. I applied for such a posting to the Provost Marshal who approved my application. In July 1943, I was ordered to report to Combined Operations at Larges on the West Coast of Scotland. I did a course of training with the Royal Marine Commandos at a school in Renfrew Road, Paisley, returning to Larges with a War unsubstantiated rank of Company Sergeant Major. I served in this rank for two months but on the formation of a new military police unit of 244 company, I reverted to my previous rank having failed to complete the 180 days for full substantiated paid rank. The new company was formed to practice beach landings at Troon & Gailes on the west coast of Scotland. In October 1943, 232 company became 244 company and moved from Scotland to Bournemouth where wet and dry landings from Tank Landing craft at various beaches on the south coast of England.

In April 1944, my company, 244 Provost Company, Military Police joined the 3rd Canadian Division at Bitterne, Southampton. The camp was in a heavily wooded area and surrounded by a barbed wire fence and no one was allowed out of camp. Entertainment for the troops was essential so a large NAAFI and cinema were built. During the six weeks internment at Bitterne, General Eisenhower and General Montgomery visited us to give lectures on landing procedures, but no indication of when and where the landings would be made. At the end of May 1944, in the early hours of the morning, the whole occupants of the camp moved to Gosport on Landing Tank craft, which contained units to be used in the early beach assault, viz.: two sp tanks, units of naval and Marine Commandos, Royal Corps of Signals, Royal Engineers and Canadian assault units. I embarked on LCT 524 and on the 1st June with other LCT's grouped in the port of Southampton.

On the morning of the 4th, we were informed over the ships tannoy, that we must be prepared to leave port for an assembly area during that evening, but this order was later cancelled due to bad weather.

CHAPTER 4

D Day Return To France

At 21.00 hrs on Monday the 5th June 1944, we sailed from port and joined a vast number of craft, including large fighting vessels of the Royal Navy, which proceeded into the channel. The weather during the night deteriorated and quite a number of the landing crafts occupants were sea sick, including a young Canadian Lieutenant (Bob Thomson) who was attached to 244 company Military Police for the landings.

. At Dawn, the French coast was sighted, and the two tanks in the well of the LCT fired two smoke shells. About one minute later the LCT was rocked by an explosion at the rear portside of the craft and water was seen rising from the tank tracks in the well of the vessel. The Canadian Captain on the bridge of the craft ordered everyone to the guard rail platform of the LCT and prepare to abandon ship. The LCT was taking in water fast, and after firing two smoke and one H.E shells from each tank, orders were given to abandon ship. We dropped into about 4 feet of water and moved up Nan beach, which was under heavy fire from German six inch mortars and sniper fire. Half way towards the beach wall Lieutenant Bob Thomson went down, and together with another Sgt. of the company we managed to get him under the sea wall. It was then that I realised that he had been shot through the head and was dead. His money and effects were handed to the beach commander on Juno beach at Benerais Sur Mer, I then carried on with my section taking 327 German prisoners from an abri (shelter) in the railway station.

Owing to the loss of transport which was still on the LCT, all duties by my Military Police section had to be carried out on foot, this entailed marking out areas for supplies by any means at our disposal. There were no serious hold ups and traffic control was maintained under severe pressure for 48 hours from the initial landings. Several fields adjacent to the beaches were mined and flail tanks had to be called in to clear them before the fields could be used for incoming supplies of ammunition and R.A.O.C. stores.

Units of the Canadian 3rd Division were held up South of the beach area, by persistent 88 mm guns situated in a wood, and the 8th brigade Canadian heavy artillery battery was bought into action, and after salvoes from 25 pound shells the 88 mm were silenced. Later as I approached crossroads on the main Caen to Bayeux road, with a corporal from my unit, a French Canadian unit of infantry signalled me to take cover, as they were under fire from a Spandua machine gun. I went to ground, so did my

Benieres-sur-mer, photograph taken prior to the "D" Day landings. Photograph found after heavy shelling of the village 6th June, 1944.

8.30 a.m. "D" Day 6th June, 1944. Landed on Juno Beach at Benieres-sur-mer, Calvados, with 48 Commando, in front of Landing Craft of 3rd Division, Canadians. Copies of photographs picked up in street outside of buildings damaged or destroyed during the shelling of the village on landing.

corporal as the Spandua machine gun took the top of a five barred gate close to where we had passed. During the morning, I accompanied a D.U.K.W. (an Amphibious Vehicle) to a stores area, which had been cleared of mine by a flail tank. On my return to the beach area, I saw a large crater in a field and saw three bodies in field grey uniforms, one of which showed slight movement. Two of the three were dead, but the third was alive, but severely wounded. Together with the R.A.S.C. driver of the D.U.K.W. we managed to get the German soldier onto the front of the vehicle, but on returning to the F.D.S (field dressing station) on the beach the man had died. Amongst items of clothing found in other debris at the bottom of the crater was an unused diary printed in German and purchased in Paris in late 1943, which I used from D Day until the end of 1944 to record daily incidents, extracts of which I have specified in the following daily order:

June 6th   Late in the day beach area shelled continuously, during the night 307 prisoners, including snipers were collected and removed to a P.O.W assembly area to be transported to U.K. by landing craft dispersing Canadian troops at that time for action stations to the south of the beach

7th   Pockets of resistance continued on D plus one many more prisoners, including snipers surrendered from houses in Benaires, Corporal Bradley was wounded in the leg from a sniper's bullet and removed to F.D.S for treatment.

8th   Came under fire from the church steeple in Benaires. Together with two corporals from my unit assisted in return fire, with members of Canadian troops of the Winnipeg rifles, of the 8th brigade artillery. Snipers both French surrendered: a boy of 16 and a girl of about the same age. They were handed over to intelligence corps personnel for interrogation.

9th   Checked points and traffic control positions on the first and second laterals, to ensure smooth flow to forward areas. Collected two prisoners from 88 mm gun site, one wounded, and removed to field dressing station near beach head. Bombing by American B17's on enemy positions south of the beach head. Shelling of the beach area at dusk, and bombing raids on the area during the night

10th   Morning raid by Messersmitts 109's but Anti Aircraft fire from Navy ships and ground fire from Anti Aircraft guns of Canadian artillery caused them to abandon the raid with no casualties in the area.

11th   French civilians appear to be bewildered and scared, and panic from intermittent shelling of Benaires Sur Mer. My section is very tired having been on duty since landing, and as no reinforcements have arrived (having been delayed by bad weather) I am compelled to take hard rations to them to consume on duty.

12th   General Montgomery visited beach at Benaires Sur Mer asked questions on traffic control and movement of stores to assembly areas south of the village.

13th   Prime Minister, Mr. Churchill, General Sir Alanbrook, and General Smuts arrived on Juno beach. Transport moving to the front smoothly, congratulated on the efforts of Military Police for quick removal of obstructions when hold ups have occurred.

14th   Charles De Gaulle arrived at the beachhead. French people jubilant. Enemy aircraft in large numbers attacked the beach area. Four bombers shot down two in the sea.

15th   Night attack by enemy aircraft on the beachhead ack ack terrific. Four German aircraft shot down, some of the crews parachuted into the sea, picked up by naval craft, and brought ashore for interrogation by beach headquarters IC.

16th   Very busy in beach Maintenance area, tanks & heavy guns unloaded, 15th Scottish, and 11th armoured divisions ashore with all equipment. Escorted by 68 section C.M.P. To assembly

Subject : Exercise "OVERLORD south of Benaires.
Headquarters,   R/
3/2.
No, 8 Beach Group.
24 Jun. 44.

Refce BG/25/2 dated 20 Jun. 44   Herewith report as requested.

Landing Priorities

Strength of Company at assault, discounting Residues, to be landed was
Personnel 73, Vehicles 10.

It was laid down in the Landing Tables that 26 of the above were to land up to
H+75 mins. Without vehicles. This, from the start, meant that the Company
was entering the operation at a disadvantage. A considerable area had to be
signed on foot, and, as battle did not go forward to time, the recce, and subse-
quent signing was hampered still further.
The remainder or bulk of the Company were due in at roughly 1200hrs. on 'D'
Day but owing to unforeseen circumstances they did not arrive until 1200hrs. on
D+1. The area therefore, that by H+12 had enlarged, still had to be signed and
pointed by the original 26 men, still without transport. The disadvantages were
enormous. Original planning for the allocation of ready made signs was such
that, instead of signs for the area beyond the first lateral being brought in at
1200hrs. on 'D' Day the last resort, previously planned had to be adopted. That
was the men going round with paint and brush, and signing as best they could.
Many complaints were lodged by certain Officers re the lack of signs but the
signs that were used, apart from a few I personally brought in a beach group
vehicle were carried in by the 26 men landing on 'D' Day. This included about
60 large 6' x 4' signs with 7' poles. However, the traffic was kept moving and at
no time, after H+120 mins, was there a serious block that was not cleared in a
few minutes. On the arrival of transport the following day the improvised signs
were erected on the roads or sites chosen by dump representatives.
        The original orders that were laid down for signing the BMA were that
small signs of the improvised type, the majority of which were carried in by the
men, were to be used, the change over to France plates taking place on about
D+3 - 4.
This, however, was not apparently appreciated so far back as D+2. Even as
soon, in some cases as signs were put down we were told to provide large
boards, especially in Courseulles. Every man in the Company was working full
out, and yet, from nowhere, and contrary to all previous instructions that were
laid down, we were expected to produce these signs almost on the spot. No one
or very few people appreciated the fact that two applications of paint had to be
made and the first or background coat had to dry before the white letters could
be put on. Even with quick drying paint each large sign took six to ten hours to
complete. However, as the days went on we were able to produce these signs
and by now they are both correct and permanent.

General traffic observations

The only mentionable and serious hold-up was at the Knee Assembly Area. This 'bad spot' in the BMA was, in almost every case of a jam occurring, attributed to Pro. Many people, landing on D+1 and D+2 who were obviously not in the picture, suggested that more Pro be put to patrol the route affected (they were all on duty in any case). The actual fault lay in the fact that the beaches at Courseulles through the town and up to the assembly area, a distance of approximately just over a mile was the route employed and when the maximum number of vehicles were on that road nothing could be done to alleviate the situation especially when the head of the column was held up at the assembly area. The only way of relieving such congestion would have been to move the assembly area further inland as and when the situation permitted.

There have been many cases of minor looting and pilfering from the first day. This has been chiefly been the work of souvenir hunters who had easy access to uninhabited premises. With the arrival of the SIB and the carrying out of more patrols this has almost ceased.

General Behaviour

This has, in the main been satisfactory. The bad state of dress, general behaviour of the troops etc. which was accepted in the early stages as inevitable, still persists however in a few cases. It is obvious that the general bearing of the men in the assault phase was not in keeping with home service levels, it was not expected, and a marked improvement was noticed about D+3 onwards. It was unfortunate that a man from this Company who landed at D+40 Mins. After being on duty continually was remarked upon as being unshaven at 1020 on D+1 by someone who had just landed. Observations of this sort can cause a great deal of harm amongst the troops, especially when they have been working all out for the good of the operation. I am convinced that 95% of those landed made shaving and general cleanliness their first priority as soon as the opportunity presents itself.

General

The help afforded by Officers and O.Rs of the 144 Coy Pmr Corps is greatly appreciated both by myself and all ranks of this Company. They have been extremely helpful during very trying period and their willing assistance will be missed if and when they are sent elsewhere.

Cean, Calvados, Le 'Englise St. Pierre. Ruin of the Church in the town. 9th July, 1944.

Cean, Calvados, unidentified photograph by War correspondent. 9th July, 1944.

Cean, Calvados, unidentified photograph by War correspondent taken the day after capture by British & Canadian troops 9th July, 1944.
The main street being cleared to allow passage of convoys through to the forward area.

Beach at Benieres-Sur-Mer, photograph taken prior to 'D'-Day landings code named 'Juno' 8.30 am 6th June 1944.

8 BEACH GROUP OPERATION ORDER No 2.

Ref. Maps: 1/25,000 Sheets 37/18 S.E. and 40/18 S.W.

INFM

1, ENEMY
(a) Posns of enemy tps are liable to daily variations and are therefore enumerated, but the following tps are in the area:-

> 21 Pz Div - Low Category, about of personnel and Tanks
> 12SS Pz Div - better quality Div in every way
> Pz Lehr Div - Low Quality trp Div with few tanks
> 2 Pz Div - A better type of Div not yet committed to battle

(b) The enemy forces are closest to BERNOGRES to the S.E in the area CAEN 6268.

(c) 8 Para Div has not yet been committed and may be used against B.M.A.

2, OWN TPS

(a) 3 Cdn Inf Div are on our immediate front with three bdes up, and with 30 Corps on the right and 3 Br Inf Div on the left to the r, ORNE. 8 Corps is to the right in res and one Bde of 51st (H) Div is on our left res.

(b) 8 Beach group and AA. elements are stationed in BERNIERES area with 4 and 7 Beach Groups on the right (in areas COURSEULLES and GRAYES Sur-Mer respectively) and 6 Beach Group on the left in area LANGRUNE Sur-Mer. The area between 6 and 8 Beach Groups is undefended. These Beach Groups have orgn. Similar to own except for No4 Group which has no Inf. Bn.

(the next para is ineligible)

(c) British have air superiority over the battle area.

INTENTION

3,   8 Beach Group and trps under comd for local def will work the beaches while responsible for NAN WHITE and NAN RED sectors unless strongly threatened Bt. enemy ground action, when they will deny the sector to the enemy.

METHOD

4,   General Plan
(a) Tps will work from bivers areas in proximity of beaches and will in general deny the sector to the enemy from the vicinity of these areas.
(b) All units and sub units localities will be sited for all round defence.

5, unreadable paragraph from original documents.
ADMIN

6.   Amn. Bn amn res at   996853

7,   Sups, Drawn by corps and units as already arranged

8,   Water. All Coys. and units will hold one day's water supply in res in addn to full water bottles. Water sterilising tablets will be collected and held centrally on pl or equivalent level.

9,   Med   R.A.P. at 996854

INTERCOMN

10,   (a) Rear Beach Group HQ. 99683
        Adv Beach Group HQ. 99585

        (b) Defence will be conducted from Adv HQ.

11   Code Words

        (a) The code word for this defensive posn tp be taken up will be KUKRI.
        (b) The code word for C. Coy to attack any sector of BERNIERES will be FOXY followed by N.E.S.W etc. referring to the sector concerned - the CHURCH being considered as the centre of BERNIERES.

DETAILED METHOD
        In the event of the code word being received Sec. Sgts. will ensure that their secs are dispatched WITH ALL POSSIBLE SPEED to R.V. at 68 Sec. HQ (opp BERNIERES Church). Co-ordinated defence on the area allotted will be set up at once on the arrival of the bulk of the Coy by the senior Officer present. Pointsmen will remain on duty the whole time

DRESS
        Any dress whatever, provided Sten Guns and ammo are carried.

In the Field
Capt.
HEE/ECU
Officer Commanding
4 Jul. 44   244 HQ Provost Company, C.M.P.

49

17th	Constant shelling of beach area, ammunition dump hit, large explosion. L/Cpl Clark on crossroads blown off road, proceeded to scene narrow escape shell dropped behind my jeep, lifted onto two wheels, but still escaped with little damage. Radar station 3 miles from beach taken by Canadians. 243 prisoners taken mostly Luffwaffe personnel.
18th	Checked Radar station at Toillaville. Underground rooms 100 feet under the operations room. Quite a lot of female clothes, lip sticks etc.found. R.E. Bomb squad accompanied me, and removed booby traps from several rooms. Germans must have left in a hurry, as several bombs found were not armed.
19th	Heard the Americans were going very well and had captured several areas south of Carentan in Cherbourg peninsular. Enemy air raids over beach area on ship hit and on fire. Heavy ack ack from the ships broke up the raid.
20th	04.30 hours air raid by enemy between Courselles and Langrune two enemy planes shot down, 3 German parachutists came down and taken prisoner by patrol men of 244 company C.M.P took them in my jeep toHQ. At Langrune, One with broken ankle to F.D.S. Arrest French civilians for theft of petrol.
21st	Guns of the Belfast bombard Caen. Americans reported to be 4 miles from Cherbourg, 8 shells fall round my HQ. At Benaires several killed and wounded. Conveyed to C.C.S on the beach.
22nd	Provost personnel of 244 company move to St Aubyn. Heavy fighting by Americans in Cherbourg. 15,000 German prisoners taken. Accompanied Sergeant from Intelligence corps, arrested French subject named Andre in S Aubyn in possession of over 200 German pamphlets, and transmitting set of German manu-

facture handed to French authority for interrogation by civilian and F.S.P personnel.

23rd   Fine day 3,000 tons of stores landed by 1500 hours and still unloading. German E boats attacked our ships , and 3 set on fire. Warspite sank two and the other escaped

24th   0800 hours beach patrol at St Aubyn by jeep, found the body of Luffwaffe pilot Freeden Gunther, of Brandenberg, Germany, had been shot in the head. Appeared to have been washed up on the shore. body removed for burial. Commended by Assistant Provost Marshal, L of C for good police work in the arrest of Salvatore De-Etto for activities against members of allied forces personnel. Artillery barrage commenced at 16.30 hours and continued until 22.30 hours.

25th   B17 flying fortress made a crash landing in beach area, returning from a bombing trip near Paris. Crew of 11 taken to landing craft leaving for U.K. Given a flying jacket by a crew member as a souvenir. British artillery still active throughout the day.

26th   Terrific British artillery action up the front line commenced at 07.30 hours. Escort to supply vehicles of R.A.S.C to Tilly Harcourt. Light shelling near the convoy from German artillery but no casualties. Returned to beach area were a record 4,900 tons of supplies were landed.

27th   Arrested Private J. Baldcock, Pioneer Corps, for theft. Convoy to front line at Epron, ammunition and stores. Heavy German shelling of front positions. Convoy arrived safely.

28th   Record unloading of stores on **Nan red** beach 5,680 tons, visited military police for conference on Gold and Sword beaches. Traffic moving smoothly on all beaches. With Royal Engineers bomb disposal unit removing booby traps from houses.

29th — Escort to supply unit R.A.S.C convoy to Tilly 8th Canadian brigade assembly area. German shelling persistent from 88 mm guns in wooded position.

30th — To gazelle supplies to British 3rd division 5 miles from Caen mortar fire from Hitler Lehr division. One vehicle hit, and two men killed in convoy. Concentrated fire from British 25 pounder guns on German positions. Returned to beach area.

July 1st — Luftwaffe attacks the beachhead with ME 109' battle with Spitfire's but no aircraft appeared to be hit, and the ME's departed without any apparent targets being hit.

2nd — First women two (W.A.A.F's) arrived to collect wounded, and return to U.K. Met two French girls Ginette and Jeannete daughters of the Mayor of St Aubyn, who both spoke English.

3rd — Arrested two soldiers from the Pioneer Corps, for the theft of rations from a D.U.K.W. Detained at the town guard room at St Aubyn.

4th — Quiet day free from shelling from the enemy. Unloading on the beach area carried out without interference, and traffic moving according to schedule. At 22.30 hours Dornier bomber shot down in flames 5 bodies recovered, from the wreckage, and removed for burial.

5th — Visited French family at St Aubyn, Rue de Marchal Foch. Son in liberation section somewhere near Dijon. Supplied then with rations from surplus army packs.

Brest peninsular. 50th division beat a Bayeux eleven at football 3-1. Brittan of Everton played for the army side.

7th
Escort to Vire and Falaise area with a convoy of supplies. Orderly Sergeant no mail due to bad weather.

8th
Section on duty throughout the day support tank units continued to pass through Bayeux in increasing numbers accompanied by military police to assembly area, near Falaise.

9th
Royal Engineers erected tentage for a sergeants mess. Orderly Sergeant. Visited patrols who were detailed to control troops who had been reported by senior officers of units in rest areas as being improperly dressed and misbehaving in cafes in Bayeux. Troops given warnings but no reports submitted for disorderly conduct. No British troops involved, but Canadians received warnings.

10th
My section played soft ball with Canadian troops who were reserve troops for the 3rd Canadian division.

11th
Orderly Sgt. Called to a bar in town centre, where American soldiers, who were very drunk had shot at a Canadian officer. Both American soldiers involved were arrested, and handed over to the American military police, who took statements from the officer involved.

12th
Orders received that big push imminent on Falaise Americans moving on Argentan with a view to trapping two German divisions 21st Panzer and 10th SS armoured division. Many prisoners expected and POW camp manned.

13th
14th   15th   16th   17th &   18th
Special Duties with Special Investigation Branch in prisoner of war camp accompanied by interpreters from Intelligence Corps.

19th	German aircraft over Bayeux at 23.50 hours, no bombs dropped. Probably reconnaissance effort AA in action.
20th	At 16.30 hours met C.Q.M.S Martin from my old company (101 Provost) now with the 1st Airborne Parachute Regiment Military Police. Also visited by two members of the ATS Provost, who had been stationed in Derby.
21st	During the morning, I was approached by a person in civilian clothes who told me that his name was Johnson and his home was in Harrow England. He stated that he was a member of a RAF bomber shot down on 18th of April near Amiens. He had been befriended by a French family and on hearing of the landings in Normandy had been told by some American soldiers to report to the English military police. He still had his RAF identity tags, but was escorted to intelligence section, who verified his story after holding him for a few days before arranging for his conveyance to the UK. He had been reported as a air gunner missing on the date referred to.
22nd	Went to a hall in Bayeux to see a film showing Ivor Novello and Diana Wynard in 'Love from a stranger'.
23rd	At 12.35 hours called to an incident by a R.A.S.C. driver who was carrying refugees from the battle zone, when his vehicle had been attacked by two Americans. With two corporals from my section and arrested the two Americans. No damage was caused to the refugees, but the Americans were taken to an American military police unit who placed them in custody.
24th	Paris falls to the Americans and the Free French. News was received that Marseilles had been occupied by British troops. Grenoble also in allied hands. Supervised patrols in Bayeux during the evening.

25th	Attended a court of enquiry re: escaped prisoners A.W.O.L. from their units. Later all the prisoners arrested and conveyed to the town guardroom.
26th	Convoy with supplies to Falaise. Many German dead lying around, also some British troops who the Pioneers have not yet buried, the aftermath of a battle of some proportion in the town.
27th	Refugees from Belgium and Holland who fled from the Germans in 1940 arrived at 244 Company Military Police Headquarters, and were given food and directed to the town authorities for information.
28th	Received a parcel from Southampton containing food etc., but no indication of who the sender was. Handed to Sgt's Mess orderly for distribution.
29th	Arrested 8 deserters from the 50th Northumbria division, and the 51st Highland division (special duties).
30th	Special duties together with other units of Provost. Arrested 13 deserters from 43, 50th, and 51st divisions.
31st	Escort to 3,000 German Prisoners of war to a compound near Bayeux.
Sept. 1st	Further batch of prisoners handed over to our company by escorts from the battle front. Taken to P.O.W compound.
2nd	8 deserters arrested, of different units, to the town guardroom.
3rd	2 deserters arrested from 51st Highland division. Stated that they had lost their unit (the Black Watch) in a village in the front line placed in custody for enquires to be made by S.I.B.

61

4th	Orderly Sergeant made arrangements with the French authorities to care for Belgian and French refugees who asked for food until they could return to their homes.
5th	Orderly Sergeant. Ten male Dutch refugees reported to military police, post manned by my two corporals. They requested to join the British army to fight against the Germans. Handed over to Intelligence corps for enquires into their request.
6th	Informed that Ostend had been captured, and the Canadians had closed in on the channel ports.
7th	Orderly Sergeant arrested Heinz Bergman a German soldier, who was dressed in civilian clothes a member of the 9th Panzer Group, who had deserted from the German army during a move to Thury Harcourt on the 2nd February by his regiment. Handed over to Intelligence corps, for interrogation.
8th	Orderly Sergeant, two refugees reported to our military police post. Both were members of Polish nobility, and one spoke English. He was identified after interrogation by Intelligence as the son of General Anders. Commander of the Polish forces fighting in France for the allies.
9th	Orderly Sergeant, two escaped prisoners of war reported to the military police post, thought that they were British, as they spoke English with a peculiar accent. I sat in on the enquiry with the men and two members of the Intelligence corps. They were members of a South African unit from Cape Town, captured at Sollum North Africa 2 1/2 years ago by the Germans and sent to a camp in Northern France from which they had escaped a few days previous during the allied advance. They stayed with my unit a few days before being repatriated to the UK.

10th	Orderly Sergeant, Cafe proprietor reported trouble with British troops who were drunk. Proceeded with two members of Provost, and found that the miscreants were not British but Americans who produced knives. They were disarmed, arrested and handed over to the American military police at Insigney. Stayed with Americans overnight to provide evidence of arrest on the two men in custody.
11th	Order to proceed with convoy to a base in Belgium. Route supplied for movement on the twelfth instance.
12th	09.00 hours proceeded from map reference point near Bayeux via Caen, Liseux, Bernays to Louviers camped for the night.
13th	Left Louviers 07.30 hours, crossed the Seine at Elbeuf reached Amiens at 12.00 hours. Visited the Cathedral. Left Amiens at 14.30 hours. Arrived Arras 17.00 hours. Stayed at Suzas where I was billeted in 1940. I was given a great welcome and my section was put up for the night, and given food and facilities for which we were very grateful.
14th	Left Arras at 09.30 hours, crossed the Belgium frontier at Tournai at 11.00 hours, and arrived at Renaix at 17.00 hours, where I met a manager of a Textile unit whom I had met in 1940. He made arrangements to allow my section to stay the night in his, and a friends house. I gave orders for my section to meet at my friends house at 09.00 hours the next morning to proceed on our journey. Such was the welcome given by the Belgians, that I and my two corporals had to round up the section and proceed on our route one hour later than that arranged. Arrived at Brussels at 11.00 hours and eventually reached Antwerp at 12.00 hours. The welcome in the city was beyond belief, and everyone was very kind.

15th	Accompanied by Major Bowey, Town Mayor to the agency maritime at 09.00. hour. to confer with Maurice De Potter, chief of the Antwerp police on a joint policing by the Military Police and with the civilian police of the city, parts of which, included Mersham, which were still in Germans occupation. Intermittent shelling of the city still continued from across the Scheldt. To avoid civilian casualties a curfew was arranged from 21.00 hours until 0600 hours. During which a Military Police combined with civilian police patrols would cover the city. All patrols being armed as arranged.
16th	244 company were settled in billets in the Vesting Straat. During the morning a number of men with National coloured armbands (members of the Belgian resistance movement) arrived in Vesting Straat, and entered a cafe opposite to the Military Police billets, and dragged onto the street three girls (later found to have been collaborators with the Germans). Their heads were shaved, and a swastika painted in black paint onto the door of the cafe. During the incident several of my men requested that we should interfere, but the request was refused as these incidents were occurring in several districts of the city, and were considered retributory acts and subject to civilian control. At 22.20 hours the city was shelled by German artillery and several civilians were killed.
17th	The post at Vesting Straat was visited during the morning by civilians making enquires of what they were expected to do in the circumstances to assist the military forces. One of the resistance party who spoke perfect English was retained at the post. His name was Van Pierre, who was regarded by the Belgians as a hero, who had recently escaped from Breendonk Concentration Camp, where he had been incarcerated in 1943 for assisting allied airmen to escape to France through a resistance network. He proved to be a valuable asset in dealing with

enquires by civilians. Van Pierre invited me to his home during the evening and showed me RAF uniforms, and one Polish Air Force jacket which he kept as a souvenirs. During his imprisonment in the Concentration Camp the finger nails on both hands had been pulled out, and when he pulled off his shirt many weal's were seen, some so deep that they were permanent. We became good friends during my stay in Antwerp, and everywhere he went people recognised him.

18th	LCpl. Taylor promoted to Sgt. Took charge of my section of 244 company, and I was attached to Special Investigation Branch to liaise with Inspector D, Van d Bergh of the Surete as my interpreter on civilian and military crime. Reports direct to Maurice De Potter, Commissioner at Surete Headquarters, National Straat, Antwerp, and to town mayor, Provost where military personnel were involved.
19th	Reported to Charlotte Lei HQ of S.I.B under Major Purslow. Investigation duties due to backlog of major crimes, many incidents due to military personnel being worse for drink, the most serious of the crimes reported were from shops in the centre of the city, and the fact that the city had become a rest area for front line troops.
20th	21st, 22nd, 23rd, 24th, 25th, 26th, with S.I.B
27th	Returned to Provost to set up a training school for recruits from other units, including A.T.S for military police duties, as replacements for C.M.P personnel who had become casualties on front line duties.
28th	Returned to duty with 244 company at Isobella Lei after a period with the Special Investigation Branch in Charlotte Lei.

29th	Mortar fire on the Docks from Merxham.
30th	Canadians take towns in the north west areas of Belgium, and consolidate with backup reserves from the 8th Canadian Brigade.
Oct. 1st	Information received from a cafe proprietor that a soldier named Frank, believed to be a Canadian was hiding up, with a prostitute in red light district of the Palingbrug Straat near the docks. Arrested at 20.00 hours as a deserter and conveyed to the Canadian Guard room in Pelikaan Straat.
2nd	Evidence of arrest of Michael Goulet, Royal Canadian Ordnance Corps at a Field General Court Marshal at Liege, charged with attempted murder of a civilian police officer in Brussels, and escaping whilst in custody from Canadian Guardroom in The Pelican Straat Antwerp.
3rd	Supervised patrols of recruits from UK sent out to replace injured personnel.
4th	Swimming at the baths in Neviere Straat, with the rest of 244 company, proprietor would not except payment.
5th	Michael Goulet reported as having escaped again and believed to be in cafe in the Suikerei. Proceeded to the place in question, and arrested Goulet, who put up strong resistance, and when searched was found to have a loaded .38 revolver in his possession. Conveyed to the Canadian guard room and handed over to Sgt. Clearwater, Royal Canadian Military Police who belonged to the Royal Canadian Mounted Police as a serving peacetime officer. Sgt. Clearwater recognised Goulet as a criminal wanted in Canada for major crimes and whose real name was Le Blanc.
6th	22.00 hours disturbance reported at a cafe in the Schoonberg Straat in Antwerp. Proceeding

Photograph obtained from underground bunker, at Taillaville on 18th June, 1944. Germans deserted the post used as a Radar Station. The bunker was booby trapped, and cleared by Royal Engineers before entry was permitted.

Photograph taken by a member of 244 Company, Military Police decending on Antwerp in December, 1944.

Photograph obtained from a captured enemy camp at Tilly Harcourt 26th June, 1944.

to the cafe referred to and found two Canadians shooting at bottles of spirits behind the bar.
The Canadian Military Police were called and
took the men into custody, after reassuring the
cafe proprietor that damage would be assessed
and the soldiers made to pay.

7th — Enquires into ration discrepancies at a D.I.D
(Royal Army Service Corps) Dept.

8th — Attended Church service at Anglican Church
in Antwerp.

9th — Called by W/T from corporal Laird on the information post Keyser Lei he had detained a
captain of the Royal Canadian Ordnance Corps
who had produced an officers identity card
(2606) from which the photograph of the owner
had been removed. I went to the post with a
Sgt. of the Intelligence Corps, and after a long
period of interrogation learned that the soldier
was private Robb of the Royal Canadian Ordnance Corps. He was detained and charged with
masquerading as an officer and theft of army
equipment.

10th — Statement by corporal Laird to the Canadian
Provost Officer on the circumstances leading
to the arrest and detention of private Robb as
detailed on the 9th inst.

11th — Supervised patrols in the city centre viz: Keyser
Lei, Koningan & Astrid Plien, Appleman Straat,
Pelican Straat, Quellen Straat, and the Staadt
Park area.

12th — Met Raoul Permeke, Antwerp business man,
who spoke very good English and volunteered
his services as an interpreter. This was approved
by the Town Mayor (Major Cowie) to cope with
the numerous enquires from Flemish speaking
public.

13th — 11.00 hours first flying bomb fell near museum,

on the schilders Straat. proceeded with members of 244 provost company assisted Antwerp police, Ambulance & Fire Brigade in rescue operations. There were many people killed and injured. The Museum was used as a collecting point for the injured. A shift system was arranged, with military police to assist at all Similar incidents if attacks continued. The authorisation for rescue operations was issued by the base commander for 244 company to carry out rescue duties in addition to normal military requirements.

14th   Four flying bombs fell on the city today, damage to property extensive and many casualties. Assistance by military personnel, organised by military police, and civilian authorities.

15th   Six flying bombs fell on the city. Each incident has now become routine, but has placed excessive demands on our resources, and patrols have now become isolated duties in view of the predominant task of rescue etc.

16th   Eight bombs fell on the city today.

17th   Five bombs fell on the city and outskirts today.

18th   Seven bombs today

19th   Seven flying bombs on various districts of the city near the south station, Boomser Steenweg, and other central parts of the city.

20th   At 23.00 hours no bombs had fallen and the city had remained quiet, except for clearing up the amounts of debris from bombed streets, were falling bricks and broken glass lay everywhere. Morale amongst the civilian population was very low and quite a number of the civilian population were leaving the city for the safety of their children.

21st   The first flying bomb dropped at 10.15 hours

and three more during the afternoon. Went to the Palace Cinema during the evening, showing a film starring Ramon Navarro.

22nd   Four V.1 bombs dropped (one near the USA 9th Army military police HQ. on the Pelikaan Straat).

23rd   First bomb fell at 09.30 hours. Proceeded to the incident. House on fire being dealt with by Antwerp Fire Brigade two people killed, several people injured. At 11.05 hours another bomb fell in the docks area, superficial damage to warehouse only casualties were from cuts from flying glass and blast shock. Returned to billets mess bill paid.

24th, 25th, 26th During these days 24 flying bombs dropped inflicting tremendous damage to building and fatalities were many, several military personnel were conveyed to the British 9th General military hospital.

27th   Five bombs on various parts of the city. Reports of many of the bombs being destroyed by AA fire, or by fighter aircraft. The civilian population are under terrific strain and the constant explosions in the city do nothing for their morale.

28th   Due to flying bomb damage and the casualties arrangements are being made for the evacuation of civilian women and children away from the city, including the elderly. Persons responsible for the daily functions for routine tasks of maintenance viz: police, fire, ambulance and hospital staff plus business staff are requested to remain.

29th   Nine flying bombs fell on the city at intervals during the day. The task of assisting the civil authorities becomes more demanding, and although it is becoming paramount and necessary.

71

| 30th | Captain Ellsmore my old company commander visited my section headquarters at 11.00 hours and had a long chat on incidents that had occurred since leaving the beach area. |

31st to the 2nd of November Eighteen flying bombs fell during this period. Six V.1s fell today. CMP dance at Isobella Lei during the evening, dance finished at 23.00 hours.

| 3rd and 4th | Fourteen flying bombs fell during the last two days. |

| 5th | Flushing captured. |

| 6th | Five flying bombs dropped. Severe damage to our HQ building. Several of the staff including myself and two other Sgt's who were in the Mess had a few cuts and bruising. Took R.S.M Hogan to St Pierres Hospital, Brussels, with head injury caused through falling masonry. |

| 7th | Middleberg and Walkeren island captured by 52nd division (my old division). |

| 8th to 24th | One hundred and nine flying bombs fell on the city and districts causing enormous damage to property and civil casualties are estimated in the thousands killed and injured. The 9th general hospital dealt with a large number of military personnel. It is now considered that the Germans are making a big effort to put the port of Antwerp out of action to delay our supply position. |

| 25th | Received a letter from Olive Moss who I saw on my leave in the UK. Together with a mate from the 1st Airborne, had tea with Mrs. Moss of Portland Street Derby last March. |

| 26th | In charge of church parade to the Anglican church Antwerp. Between 13.00 hours and 23.00 hours seventeen flying bombs fell on the |

city of Antwerp and district. Assisted civil police, local ambulance and hospital staff in the rescue efforts sorting debris for dead and injured.

27th

CMP information post destroyed by V2 five military police casualties two dead, three injured, Injured included corporal Cadwood both legs amputated, L/Cpl Hill to 9th general hospital with severe internal injuries.

28th

Port of Antwerp opened today to enable supply ships to unload and facilitate new routes to be opened for front line operations. Nine flying bombs fell on the city during the day. Antwerp became the most unhealthy place behind the front line. An incessant stream of V1 and V2 bombs rained down upon it. They came at a rate described in the day-to-day German diary completed up to the end of 1944. The target area was small and considerable damage and loss of life were caused as the bombing continued thought out the night and little sleep was possible. Antwerp Garrison came under a lot of strain. On the 27th of November, a V2 fell just outside the information post of Military Police Corps. NCOs of 244 company were on duty at the post. Two were killed and eight were wounded. One of those killed was never found. Many civillians were either killed or injured M DE Potter, commissioner of Police was most impressed by the efficient and kind organisation provided by the civilian services, and most grateful for assistance of the Military Police. On the 5th of May 1945, the German Army surrendered at Lunerburg Heath. The Military Detachment which commanded the commander in Chiefs tactical HQ. Throughout the campaign conducted the German delegation to Field Marshal Montgomery, who said The Battle of Normandy would never have been won but for the work, application and cooperation of the Military Police.

29th	Martin's house destroyed by a V1 bomb. His wife and children were not in at the time.
30th to 5th	of December. Twenty nine flying bombs fell on the city and districts.
6th	Attended the wedding of Lieutenant Van de Bergh. Five bombs fell today.
7th	A party was held at the home of Jan. Pieters 624 Groote Steenweg, to celebrate the wedding of Van de Bergh.
8th and 9th	Eleven flying bombs fell on the city and districts today.
10th	Went to Anvers Palace with the daughter of Van de Bergh, to see the film "Battle of Britain". Five flying bombs fell today.
11th	Orderly Sgt. 244 company. Van de Bergh's daughter commenced duty as clerk to Captain Green. Very good typist, and speaks very good English.
12th	Temporary posting to Special Investigation Branch, in Charlotte Lei, under Captain H. Purslow.
13th	Special Duties in the Kuiper Straat, on observation of suspect soldiers living with prostitutes and being absent without leave.
14th	Arrested Frank O'Connell (A.W.O.L.) leaving a house in Kuiper Straat with a prostitute. Member of Royal Canadian Artillery. To Canadian Guard Room.
15th	Arrested Private Mc Allister Kings Own Scottish Borders for the theft of a gold watch from a shop on the Keyser Lei.
16th	Accompanied by Lt. Van de Bergh. Surete,

Antwerp Police. Visited a cafe in Mersele, where it was alleged British soldiers had been poisoned by the sale of illicit liquor. Further enquires were made at a farm at Vendoom, where a still was found under the floorboards of one of the farms outbuildings. Farmer arrested and taken to Civil Police building on National Straat, Antwerp. Statements taken from the soldiers, to be used as evidence.

17th   Together with other members of the Special Investigation Branch, arrested twenty seven members of a Royal Engineers unit, stationed at Poligon Camp for the theft of Government Stores and disposal to Civilian outlets.

18th   Together with other members of the S.I.B and two members of the civilian police Inspectors Van de Bergh and Van Dyke. We arrested two members of H.M, Forces, involved with eight business men from Belgium and Holland who were involved in currency & diamond deals. Recovered diamonds, 8,000 Dutch Guilder, 6,000,000 Belgian Francs, from premises on Pelikaan Straat and Vestry Straat.

19th   Statements taken in support of evidence in connection with arrests made on the 18th. Accompanied by Lt. Van de Bergh visited a small shop on Yser Straat, where the proprietor admitted receiving a gold watch from Private Mc Allister on the morning of the 14th December.

20th   V1 dropped in the garden of Provost company. The rear of the building completely demolished. A Sgt. from the R.E.M.E. and I were in the Sgt's Mess both slightly injured by falling masonry. Nine other military policemen also injured but none seriously.

21st   Took Captain Purslow to Antwerp Central Railway Station with two heavy suit cases, after seeing him on the train, I returned to S.I.B headquarters. At 18.00 hours proceeded to a shop of Nellens on the Mecklesur Steenweg and had tea with the family.

22nd Further enquires and observation with Sgt. House S.I.B on a ship on the River Schelde, which had a river barge tied alongside. Saw several crates unloaded from the hold of the ship, onto the barge, which the harbour master identified as a Dutch barge from Terneuzen.

23rd Sgt. House and I, went to a house in Terneuzen. Contacted the civil police who proceeded to the barge docking area where at 19.00 hours, we saw the barge seen on the Schelde the day previously. Went on board with the civil police and after a search of the hold found six cases of English cigarettes, with labels attached consigned to the NAAFI, with the port of unloading at Antwerp docks. The civil police took the barge captain his wife and two daughters into custody, and charged them with theft. Copies of statements were taken with a view to making further enquires, into the collusion by merchant shipping staff. These enquires to be made by harbour police. Returned to Antwerp at 23.00 hours.

24th Sgt. House and I to investigate the disposal of the cigarettes source together with the Dutch police, and to arrange for the transfer to the NAAFI premises of the stolen cigarettes in Antwerp.

25th During the evening, and through the night 119 flying bombs fell on the city. Everything was chaotic, and the death and injury toll was horrific. All services civil and military police, ambulance and hospital staff worked throughout the night recovering bodies of dead and injured from extensively damaged properties.

26th, 27th, 28th Special duties with investigation branch of military police investigating the problem of soldiers deserting their units and hiding in the city area.

29th Returned to duty for convoy work on lines of

	communication from the increasing amount of stores entering the port for the front line.
30th	Convoy to Tilborg Holland, for supply dump in rear headquarters to the front line. Returned to Antwerp early hours of the 31st.
31st	Assembly point in the dock area for directional location point for convoys. Completed German diary for 1944.

During the morning of the 1st January 1945 the city was attacked by German aircraft and several were shot down, I received a telephone call from a Belgian civilian, who reported that one of the planes had come down in the Schelde, and the crew were still in the aircraft. I went to the point described with our R.E.M.E.Sgt. and two members of 244 company. On arrival the aircraft lay on the bank of the river, but the canopy was bent. The R.E.M.E. Sgt. released the canopy and the crew of two were extricated. One of the crew was slightly injured, but the pilot appeared to be unarmed. The pilot was taken to the headquarters of the intelligence corps for interrogation. The other member of the crew was taken under military police escort to 109 military hospital in Antwerp. With regular supplies to forward operational units in demand the duties of 244 company were varied consisting with patrols and attending to incidents connected to the V1s and V2 (rockets) that fell in and on the outskirts of the city. It was to ease the plight of my company, who were dealing with the rescue, of civilian and service personnel, injured and dead in bomb incidents that off duty periods for the company, would be required to rest and sleep, as very little pleasure was possible under the very stressful circumstances.

As the advance of the Army towards the Rhine continued, bomb sites in Holland and France were captured, and the daily flying bombs on Antwerp were reduced. Dances were arranged at the 21 Club and civilian females invited, a dance was arranged by members of a committee at another venue that organised a dance particularly for members of the Corps of Military Police. It was at one of these functions that I met a young widow, and during the period of our friendship, I learned that she had lost her husband during the German occupation. She had her own flat and after the death of her husband, she had been employed during the latter part of the war in a menial position. This was below her standard of education and ability. It was not until the allied forces took the city from the Germans that she was able to take up suitable employment with a business firm in the city centre. She spoke several languages, both of her parents had been interrogated by Gestapo agents for supplying food to a Jewish family. Her father was a diamond cutter and her mother was one of the finest women that I had ever met. I learnt that the girl who I had met was educated at a boarding college near Brussels called Wavre Notre Dam. We talked about our lives and found that the similarity was uncanny we had both lost our partners during the war and as a result we spent a lot of time in each other company.

With the port of Antwerp open on the 27th November 1944, the supply route to the forward troops developed, and convoy duties were becoming part of a plan route for lines of communications west of the Rhine, Wesel became the first British crossing of the river whilst American troops had crossed the Rhine near Bonn. During the last days of January 1945, I was attached to the S.I.B, to assist in investigation of thefts and other offences committed by soldiers in the Antwerp area. During this period of liaison with the civilian police (Surete) became a great success and the joint venture, reduced criminal activity to a minimum. My interpreter was Inspector Van de Burgh and he was present during all investigations. I returned to normal duties by introducing a training school for intakes from the light artillery personnel from gun sights both male and females (ATS) who had volunteered to become Military Police recruits. Two of the female staff trained at Antwerp training school, one a sergeant, took part in the trials of Nazi war crimes in Nuremberg. After training several squads to bring the Corps up to the required strength I returned to 244 company and continued convoy duties on lines of communication.

It was on one of these convoys that I received serious leg injuries and was flown back to the United Kingdom. The ambulance plane was a DC3 which eventually touched down at Lynham in Wiltshire, later being entrained at Swindon for a journey across country to a military hospital at Newmarket. For three months I was kept on a blood transfusion and saline solution drip, with the possibility of amputation of the leg. I was at Newmarket for 12 months before transfer to Bury St Edmonds. After thirteen operations to the leg, I was transferred to Etwall, Derbyshire for convalescence. During the whole period of hospitalisation, I received correspondence with my girl friend in Belgium, and after my transfer from Etwall to Parwich convalescent home I accepted an invitation to visit her home. I obtained a months leave from the doctors at Parwich, and succeeded in reaching Antwerp on crutches. I was given a great time, and eventually (after my discharge from hospital) we were married in Derby in October 1946. In the early period of 1947, I attended the Derbyshire Royal Infirmary for continued treatment on my left leg, which was shortened by one and a half inches. I also attended the Sherwood hospital Nottingham for special shoe fitting.

In my period of service with the Corps of Military Police, I have read through many historical books from Dunkirk to D Day and from D Day to the surrender of the German Army at Lunerburg Heath. In no index of operation branches have the units of Provost been mentioned. The secrecy surrounding the SAS must be Equivalent.

Photograph of War casualties in convalesence after long periods in Military Hospitals at Parwich, 1946. Most of the casualties were from the Derby & Nottingham Districts. *Author shown seventh from the left on the back row.*

Shortly after cessation of hostilities Major S.F. Crozier MBE, wrote an article in a national newspaper in which Sir Miles Dempsey, Commandant of the Royal Military Police , better known as the General Officer Commanding the 2nd Army, which pushed the Germans from Normandy to the Rhine. He unveiled a memorial to the 900 Officers and Men of the Royal Military Police killed between 1939 and 1945. The Memorial was unveiled at Inkerman Barracks Woking. The fatalities, like other soldiers who lost their lives on active service died for this country's cause but, by the manner of their deaths, they did something else as well: ***They changed the army's contempt for the Military Police into respect and even admiration.*** Most of them were killed in battle, marking lanes through mine fields, on the beaches, or on heavily shelled crossroads. The order had been reserved. The Red Caps were in front of the troops not behind them. Lest there are any arm chair soldiers who still suppose that Military Police are to be found in comfortable billets at base. Here are some instances of how they died: At Calais, where the Garrison was ordered to fight to the last. Two Military Policemen volunteered to take a message through the encircled German Lines. One was killed and the other got through. He reported that when he last saw his comrades in Calaise they were fighting side by side with the rifle brigade. At Hermanville just behind the Normandy beaches there was an important crossroads. The Red Cap who controlled the flow of traffic was blown to pieces by enemy shell fire. So were all of his successors until the enemy battery was silenced, but no Army Vehicle ever lost its way at the crossroads. For as one Military Policeman fell another took his place. The men who went out to that traffic point knew they would probably not get back. They did not shelter in a ditch or trench, for a traffic policeman you cannot see is not much use, they just went out to do their duty and died.

One morning when Caen had fallen, but was still under constant shell fire from the Germans, a military policeman stood on point duty outside the town, during the afternoon his relief found him dead at his post. He had not sought shelter in a ruined building near his post, as shelter. He had by his presence on the road prevented careless troops from death by shelling, or disease, as the area was covered with corpses, because unburied bodies were subjected to disease. The infantry and tank crews, who, in battle risk death every minute could consider the MP's lot as trifling, but if they had been asked to discard their armour and trenches and stand unprotected on a crossroads under constant shell fire, I think they would agree it takes a pretty cool sort of courage.

If the R.M.P. had a motto it might well have been "First in" "Last out". When the BEF were retiring from France an infantry platoon holding the perimeter round Dunkirk noticed a section of Military Police putting up signs for the troops to follow. It seemed that the Red Caps were making for the beaches first they roundly abused them. The Policemen being quite use to that sort of thing ignored the comments. Next day the troops passed through the perimeter guided by the police signs. The Infantrymen were about to retire themselves when they noticed the same Military Police section riding back towards the Germans to collect signs and equipment. On Dunkirk beaches the Provost companies of the RMP did not leave with the other remaining troops, but stayed behind to Marshal the remaining troops to the boats. The last boat to leave contained many Red Caps, and many more bodies of Red Caps were left behind killed at their posts.

On D Day they formed part of the Beach Groups disembarking from landing craft with commando units. Their objectives were to control the movement of men and equipment to the assembly point. The German resistance anything like this happened again he would be dismissed. Some days later he came to my office and informed me that he had told his parents of the incident, and felt that some stigma would remain if he stayed with the company. He told me that he was going to join the army and asked me if his actions with the torch and stop watch would impede him joining the forces I told him that he had only had a verbal reprimand and that was the end of the matter, there was nothing on his work record, and I wished him luck.

There were many more incidents that I could include but it would make for very heavy reading.

Before retiring from Courtaulds, I was introduced to Jack Mc Grath, manager of Uttoxeter Race Course and he offered me the position of part-time Security Officer with the National Hunt Racing Section. I accepted the offer and attended my first meeting in 1969. I was detailed to patrol the stables, I was also informed that only the trainers and head stable lads were allowed inside the horse boxes due to the doping of horses at that time. The Security Staff at all National Hunt meetings were ex-police officers. After three meetings at Uttoxeter, I was given the opportunity of attending race meetings at Southwell, Stratford-on-Avon, Warwick and Pontefract with various tasks which included, the checking of badges for the club enclosure, jockeys weighting in entrance, and supervising the turnstiles for the admission of the general public to the course. The long journeys to and from race meetings put quite a pressure on my home life and reluctantly I retired from National Hunt employment in 1972.

After some two months of unemployment, I was walking down Sadler Gate, when I bumped into one of the senior partners of a local solicitors firm. After talking for some time, I was asked if I would consider talking on a part-time position as a filing clerk covering the following areas of probate, marital, conveyancing and litigation. I remained in their employment until 1987.

Between my part-time employment, my wife and I visited many ancestral homes, including Chatsworth House, and developed an interest in collecting paintings and water colours, 18th and 19th century pottery and porcelain. We have studied many books on the subject and now have quite a collection.

In 1980, I met a Mrs. Marson who lived in Spondon, after talking to her, I found out that her husband's father had served in the Grenadier Guards in around 1879 during the Boer War and Egyptian campaigns as a Sgt. I told Mrs. Marson that my grandfather Thomas Thorn had also served with the regiment as a C/Sgt. in both of these campaigns. Mrs. Marson left Spondon in 1986 to stay with relatives in the south of England, but before leaving she offered me a silver watch that had belonged to her husband's father. I said that I would purchase the watch from her, she said she did not want anything for it, but I felt that I should give her something and gave her £25.00 for it. Inscribed on the inside of the case were these words: Sergeant C. Marson, 2nd Battalion Grenadier Guards. The assay mark denoting the year as 1879/80. The watch is still in my possession, and in working order.

In 1994, I had an accident in my car, which broke my neck, luckily for me I was not paralysed. Since being born in 1910 it is always easy to remember my age, but, I am still enjoying life to the full.

Photograph taken of the Victory in Europe parade in May, 1995. Although physically
unable to take an active part, due to war disablement,
I was privilaged to attend the celebrations